Black and White and Red All Over

BLACK AND WHITE
AND RED ALL OVER

The Story of a Friendship

———

Martha McNeil Hamilton

and Warren Brown

PublicAffairs
New York

Published in the United States by PublicAffairs™,
a member of the Perseus Books Group.

Book design by Mark McGarry, Texas Type & Book Works, Inc.
Set in Dante

Library of Congress Cataloging-in-Publication data
Hamilton, Martha McNeil.
Black and white and red all over / Martha McNeil Hamilton and Warren Brown. — 1st ed.
p. cm.   Includes index.
ISBN 1-58648-156-8
1. United States—Race relations—Case studies. 2. Friendship—United States—Case studies.
3. Donations of organs, tissues, etc.—United States—Case studies. 4. Hamilton, Martha
McNeil. 5. White women—United States—Biography. 6. Brown, Warren, 1948– 7. African
American men—Biography. 8. Washington post (Washington, D.C.: 1974) 9. Washington
region—Biography. 10. Houston (Tex.)—Biography. 11. New Orleans (La.)—Biography.
I. Brown, Warren, 1948– II. Title.
E184.A1 H216 2002
305.8'00973—dc21
2002030687

FIRST EDITION
10 9 8 7 6 5 4 3 2 1

Contents

Prologue

November 20, 2001

Martha's Story

Festive.

I know it's odd, but that's how it seemed the morning of the kidney transplant.

It was cold and dark outside when we arrived at a nearly deserted Georgetown University Hospital for the surgery. If we had to be there at 5:30 A.M., why didn't the staff? No one was there to check us in, but I signed in dutifully at the empty desk.

My daughter Sarah and I were first to arrive, followed soon after by *Washington Post* photographer Michael Williamson. Then a car pulled up outside, and Warren and his family joined us. By the time our whole contingent was there, the mood in the waiting room felt social and convivial. We were all introducing ourselves and chatting and joking when they called my name.

Warren had told me, the organ donor goes first.

Sarah followed me back to the surgical prep area, a corridor of curtained-off changing rooms. Out of the jeans and a worn, cotton turtleneck and into the faded blue, print hospital gown. I settled into the comfortable chair in the cubicle, bundled in a heated blue blanket.

Across the way I could hear Warren and his family being led to his cubicle and Michael tagging along with his camera. A few minutes later, dressed for the operating room, we opened the curtains so we could chat across the way.

It was Tuesday, November 20, 2001. It had been just over three months since Warren's rapidly declining health and rising fear had prompted me to offer him one of my kidneys for a second transplant. Warren's life had been hanging in the balance since 1995, when his kidneys began shutting down, setting him on a medical course with the ominous name "end-stage renal disease."

Two years ago, Warren's wife Mary Anne had been the organ donor. But a virus had destroyed the transplanted kidney. Now, she was sitting beside Warren in the cubicle, slumped in a chair with her head on her hand. Mary Anne looked exhausted and on the verge of tears.

It had been a tough fall. Against the backdrop of the terrorist attack on September 11, Warren and I and our families also had struggled through a series of medical tests and the anxiety of surgery scheduled and then canceled. Poked and prodded and anxious to have the procedure over and done with, I found myself waking up in the predawn hours in the weeks between September 11 and the day of the surgery, startled into alertness by the noise of fighter aircraft and helicopters overhead. And then I'd stay awake, wrestling with second thoughts. Was I doing something that I would come to regret? Helping a friend is one thing, but was I paying enough attention to the possible long-term consequences, such as the implications for my own health ten or fifteen years into the future? Despite the early morning anxieties, I always ended up in the same place: I wanted Warren to live.

At the office, well, there was something oddly workaday about the prospect of the surgery. Warren and I and our friend Frank Swoboda all sat near each other in a cluster of three desks in the newsroom at the *Washington Post*. We were close colleagues and good friends. Frank was as much a party to the surgery as Warren and I were, providing the hand-holding and counseling and laughter we needed in the weeks leading up to the operation. Conversations about the progress of my medical tests, dialysis, and Warren's slumping health wove in and out of office gossip, complaints about editors, discussions of stories, and Frank's and Warren's endless chatter about cars. Sometimes I worried. Most times I didn't. Sometimes I felt choked with fear about how sick Warren was becoming. Other times I wanted to throttle Warren for not paying enough attention to his health or to what I needed to know about the transplant.

Now, in the surgical prep area, the hospital was coming to life. Doctors and nurses and technicians hustled in and out of the cubicles—checking our vital signs and asking us questions we had already answered countless times at other steps in the process.

It was a strange place to be for someone in perfect health. I wasn't a patient, so what was I? I fell back on the role that came most naturally to me—newspaper reporter. They asked me questions; I asked them questions. Or we chatted. I asked the hospital worker who put the IV in my arm about his cap, made from fabric with an unhospital-like chili pepper print. His sister made it, he said. It was all very sociable.

After the months of waiting, it felt like a huge accomplishment to be at the hospital finally, ready for action.

Michael was taking pictures, moving back and forth from Warren's cubicle to mine. The doctors asked me if I needed a gurney or a wheelchair to go to the operating room.

———

"I can walk," I said, "unless you guys know something I don't."

Warren ducked under his blanket, covering his head to shut out the reality of what was happening, and Michael took a picture of Warren, looking like an Afghan woman in a blue burqa. Michael wanted a picture of us together, so Warren came out of hiding and I walked across the way carrying my IV bag for a pre-op picture of the two of us, in our matching blankets and blue shower caps.

I met the anesthesiologist. People stuck needles in me. There were more questions. Sarah left briefly to see if my sister, JE McNeil, had arrived. While she was gone, they wanted to move me to the operating room, but I wasn't budging until Sarah got back. Fortunately, the wait was just a few minutes. I walked to the operating room, feeling very much in control. Sarah walked with me and gave me a hug and a kiss as I headed in.

Suddenly, in the operating room, I was no longer in control. I was flat on my back. People who didn't introduce themselves were very busy moving around my body, strapping me down, paying no attention to the conscious me.

I glanced to the right, where Michael stood, taking pictures. "Let the record reflect that I'm officially nervous," I said. And that was my last conscious thought.

Warren's Story

Dying seemed preferable. No more surgery. No more pain. No more early morning visits to the dialysis center. No more fear of another kidney transplant failure. No need to depend on a loved one, or friend, to trade a part of her life to save the rest of mine.

I dreamed of a quick exit, life snipped off by the hand of God. That way, no one could charge me with suicide, a damnable sin in my Catholic faith. I couldn't be kicked out of heaven for something God did.

But the dream ended when the clock alarm sounded at 4 A.M. on November 20. Martha must be getting up about now, I thought. She's seldom late, especially for something as important as this. She was giving me another chance at life, my second kidney transplant.

Mary Anne, my wife of thirty-three years, was still asleep beside me. She always seemed so vulnerable asleep, so beautiful. I kissed her forehead. She did not stir. I sat up next to her, stroking her hair. She already had been through so much, including the death of the kidney she had given me two years ago and the subsequent death of her mother. Telling Mary Anne that I would lose her kidney was the hardest thing I've done. She invested so much of herself in saving me.

I did not want to give her another death. I was shamed by my dream of convenient demise.

So, here we were at 5:30 A.M. in the surgery waiting room of Georgetown University Hospital. I was accompanied by Mary Anne and our daughters, Binta and Kafi. Normally, I walk behind Mary Anne and the girls when we're out together, partly to guard against would-be purse snatchers, and partly because I walk at a slower pace. But this morning, I walked ahead of them. It wouldn't be good to give Martha the impression that I wanted none of this, although that is what I was thinking and feeling.

Martha, as I expected, was sitting in the waiting room already with her heart, her daughter Sarah. Martha is a tough woman, but she's doting mush in Sarah's presence.

I did not want any of us to be here. I wanted none of this and tried to wish it all away. I wanted Mary Anne to have her kidney back. I wanted Martha to keep her kidney. I did not want to be cut, to be opened up on a surgery table, ever again. I didn't want Martha to be cut. I didn't want to be on dialysis, either; and, despite my dream, I really didn't want to die.

I divorced myself from my immediate surroundings and company and sought an audience with God. It was an attempt to negotiate. Something about all of this didn't make sense. I figured that the Almighty was a reasonable dude, and that he would see things my way, if approached correctly.

But God was unavailable that early in the morning. I couldn't reach him. He didn't call back. He didn't make it all go away.

I was scared as hell. They are going to cut us, Martha. They are going to take one of your kidneys and give it to me, and it could all be for naught. This transplant could fail, too. Hell, we could both die. What we're about to do is more intimate, more dangerous, than having sex. What the hell are you smiling about?

But I gave no voice to my thoughts. I locked them in a mental panic room with the rest of my fears and misgivings.

Martha was called to the surgery preparation room a little after 6 A.M. She was remarkably calm, and that made me jealous.

"Warren Brown?" A nurse was calling me, too. I was shocked that they were asking for me so soon. When Mary Anne gave me her kidney in 1999, they had left me in the waiting room for an hour or so after she had been summoned.

But now, Martha and I were being brought in together, trailed by our families. She was smiling. I pretended to smile. While the nurses and doctors worked with Martha on the opposite side of the preparation room, I sought refuge beneath a blue hospital blanket, which I pulled over my face and head.

Negotiating with God hadn't worked. I decided to pray again anyway. Perhaps the Almighty would get the message and allow things to turn out okay for all of us.

Black and White and Red All Over

"Did Martha give you her kidney because you're black?"

It had been an interracial operation—black and white and red all over, just like the old newspaper joke.

Washington Post columnist Courtland Milloy was on the phone raising the race issue with Warren almost before the anesthesia wore off. Warren was in severe pain and confined to his hospital bed. The slightest movement caused agony. A nurse's aide had handed him the receiver.

Courtland was courteous. "How you doin', man?" and all of that. But it was Thursday. He was on deadline for a column that had to be edited for the Sunday paper. It wasn't a social call.

Courtland didn't want to scoop us—he knew we were writing about the transplant surgery for the newspaper's health section. But he was on to a part of the story we had ignored.

The transplant surgery was big news among our colleagues at the *Washington Post,* and the story was right up Courtland's alley. It was black and white and male and female. It was warm and fuzzy with an edge, the irony being the reality that the *Post* newsroom isn't much of a warm and fuzzy place. Our story said something about changing times, human values, and friendship.

We were friends who didn't see each other in black and white. Courtland's question reminded us that the rest of the world did. After the surgery and after our story appeared, much of the reaction from colleagues, friends, and people who didn't know us focused on our differences.

The questions weren't hostile, just curious. Sometimes they were as subtle as asking Martha: "What made you think that you and Warren were biologically compatible?" Other times, they were flat-out-in-your-face. "A white woman gave a black man her kidney?" a coworker's mother and aunt had both asked incredulously.

People were so accustomed to race being an obstacle in daily relationships that they were astonished that it played no role in a friendship where the bond now involved life-and-death risk.

Why didn't race matter? The philosophical answer is, because integration works. The personal answer is that we are friends. We spent most of our days, weeks, and months sitting next to each other, listening to each other's phone calls and family arguments and sympathizing with each other when times were rough. We saw each other as individuals, flaws and all. The newsroom was our community, and we were next-door neighbors who looked out for each other.

Once, that would have been impossible.

We both grew up in the racially segregated South during a time when water fountains were labeled "white" and "colored," where blacks were confined to the back of the bus and the balconies of movie theaters. When we were growing up, the laws against race-mixing might have made the transplant itself an illegal act. Even interracial blood transfusions were forbidden.

Then, we couldn't have imagined sitting together at the *Washington Post,* spending more time with one another than we spend with our respective families.

But by the time the transplant occurred, it seemed the most natural thing in the world.

Life had changed. The Civil Rights Movement had happened. Race riots had destroyed parts of large cities. Civil-rights laws had been enacted and implemented. Affirmative action had changed the face of the workplace. The *Washington Post,* in search of women and blacks in the 1970s, had hired us, and we had become friends.

Still, it wasn't that long ago when racial separation, legally enforced and culturally embraced, was the norm for the United States of America. That might have accounted for some of the astonished reaction from so many people, blacks and whites alike.

"A white woman gave a black man her kidney?"

Was it that hard to believe in that kind of friendship?

Black and White and Red All Over

[1]

Growing Up with Jim Crow

Martha's Story

I was eight years old in 1954, when the Supreme Court ruled on *Brown v. Board of Education,* a decision designed to end school segregation. Nine years later, when I graduated from Milby High School near the Houston ship channel, I had never spent one day in an integrated classroom.

I grew up in a blue-collar neighborhood in southeast Houston where everything was strictly segregated. I remember, the day after the Supreme Court ruling, the dark utterings of some of my classmates. "My mama said she'd send me to private school before she'd let me go to school with niggers," said one friend. "They don't have the money," my mother pointed out when I relayed this bit of schoolyard news.

My parents had a different take. Integration was the law of the land.

Houston and our neighborhood were full of folks like my family who had followed jobs to Texas. Many of us had kinfolk back in Mississippi, Georgia, or Louisiana, and we often returned to those states for vacations, sleeping on pallets on the floors of their houses.

But in my family, we weren't allowed to say "nigger." We would have gotten a whipping—the same as if we had said a swearword. Sure, we were southerners and proud of it. But that didn't mean we were ignorant racists. I was taught growing up that the Civil War was about states' rights, not slavery. And I grew up with a mixture of pride in being southern ("Only Yankees put sugar in their cornbread," my mother would say with great disdain if we were served offending cornbread in a cafeteria) and the sneaking suspicion that we were looked down upon.

Houston was an oil boomtown, a hot, muggy place full of bayous, mosquitoes, and industrial landscapes. The refineries and petrochemical plants were beautiful at night, lit up by the blue and orange flaring natural gas and strings of fairy lights that traced the shapes of storage tanks and exhaust towers. You could tell which way the wind was blowing when you stepped out our back door by whether the air smelled like petrochemicals, the sewage treatment plant, or the pulp mill.

My parents were different from most parents in the neighborhood. For one thing, my mother, Evelyn Sims McNeil, worked. She worked first as a stenographer, then as a substitute teacher. She ended her career as one of the most respected English teachers at our local high school, Milby, from which she also had graduated.

My parents were also different politically. In 1952, when just about all the Democrats in the neighborhood, and many of the Democrats in the state, were voting for Dwight D. Eisenhower, my parents were ardent Adlai Stevenson backers.

My daddy, Bruce McNeil, was a machinist at an oil refinery, a skilled craftsman and a strong union supporter. Both of my parents had come of political age under the spell of the Roosevelts, who were political heroes to them. They were activist Democrats and hugely more tolerant than was the norm, even if my daddy never did lose the habit of saying "nigger." We weren't allowed to say a lot of the words my daddy used.

I grew up in a white, white world. My neighborhood was segregated. The church where I went was all white. The schools stayed segregated in what was later ruled to be defiance of law. The clerks in the stores were all white. The library ladies were all white. The garbagemen were all white. But the fear of integration was palpable, and feelings were strong.

It wasn't a world of privilege. When I was a toddler, before my younger brother and sisters were born, we took in a boarder during a housing shortage. Eventually, there were five children: my older sister Laura; me; the twins, Malcolm and Margaret; and my baby sister, JE. We didn't live in a "big house"; we lived in a three-bedroom, one-bathroom house that barely accommodated our family of seven. (Daddy finally closed in our front porch to make a fourth bedroom for my brother.)

I was a tangle-headed, not-too-clean small child and had bare feet so tough that I could walk blocks on hot asphalt in a Texas July. My daddy worked extra shifts to earn time-and-a-half and double-time, and my mother pursued graduate degrees to increase her schoolteacher's pay.

Early on, I was blessed with my parents' high expectations. From the time I was the smallest child, my parents assumed that I would amount to something important. When I drew floor plans for a house as a nine-year-old, my parents thought I might become an architect. When I picked out a few bars of Haydn's "Surprise Symphony" on the piano and called my mother in to hear it, she took it for granted that I might become a composer. When I fashioned a crude system of levers out of scrap lumber in the backyard, my parents watched and declared me an engineering candidate. When I ignited my youngest sister's hair, though, they failed to see it as the safe, scientific experiment it was (she had very long hair) and just gave me a whipping.

Somehow I developed a passion to be a reporter.

It was an odd aspiration at a time when newspapers seldom hired women except as society reporters. Maybe it was in part because my daddy had swept out a newspaper office in DeQuincy, Louisiana, and had fallen in love with newspapers. My family took two newspapers, the *Houston Post* in the morning and the *Houston Press,* a Scripps Howard publication, in the afternoon. I started reading the comics, then moved on to the television reviews and advice columns. Soon I was flipping through the newspapers on a regular basis, which meant coming across the odd article that gripped my attention.

I have a faded index card, an issue of the *Pleasantville News Paper,* a newspaper that I wrote, printed (in pencil), and published at the age of nine or ten, according to my mother's notation. A tiny, two-column newspaper, it contained a single news story, headed "New School to Open." The text is concise: "Pleasantville school will open Dec. 1. The students are to come at 8:00." The newspaper's two ads are: "By your Chistmas cards at Macks [*sic*]" and "Get your books at the Book Shelf. Give a book for Christmas." There is an ambivalent lost-and-found notice. "Boy and dog," is all it says. And the filler at the bottom of the second column reads: "Love one another."

While I was falling in love with newspapers, my parents were engrossed in public affairs. One of the major news stories I remember from my childhood was a high-profile murder trial. A white woman had hired a black woman to help her find someone to kill her husband. The black woman and the black man she hired to do the job were sentenced to death. The white woman, who had set it all in motion, was sentenced to prison. My mother was outraged by the injustice.

There was also a neighborhood shooting. A holier-than-thou member of the Houston School Board, a woman we sometimes ran into at the neighborhood grocery store, shot her husband, a police lieutenant, in the abdomen with a shotgun. My mother, the teacher, was not enamored with the woman's performance on the school board and took some satisfaction in the evidence that the school board member's family wasn't perfect.

God knows, ours wasn't. My daddy was a terrific, loving man who wanted the best for his children, but, often, when he came stumbling in from the beer joints late at night, all

he remembered were his grievances. ...
legitimate ones. His dad had died when l
mother hadn't been able to care for the c
brother Malcolm and sister Dorothy v
Columbus, Georgia, to Louisiana, where they lived with an
aunt and uncle. Another brother went to live with an aunt
in New Jersey, and their baby brother was adopted by an
older half-brother.

Daddy had worked to pay his keep during the hours he
wasn't in school. It was a hard life, and it meant that high
school was the end of his academic career, although he
would have liked to go to college and law school.

When he got drunk, he could be either a very loving
man or a hard man who beat his children for real or imagi-
nary infractions. Talking back—or "mouthing off," which
was my weakness, could trigger another beating.

I would lie awake at night waiting to hear the car in the
driveway so I'd know he hadn't killed himself that night.
And then I'd wait to hear which daddy had walked in the
door. Sometimes it was the loving daddy, who would come
into the bedroom and tuck us in and sing the songs of Jim-
mie Rodgers "The Singing Brakeman" to us. I can't tell you
how many nights I fell asleep to my daddy singing: "All
around the water tank, just waiting for a train. A thousand
miles away from home, just waiting in the rain. . . . I walked

p to the brakeman, just to give him a line of talk. He said if you've got money, son, I'll see that you don't walk. . . . I have not got a penny. Not a nickel can I show. Get off, get off, you railroad bum. He slammed the boxcar door." Yodeling followed, which I do much better than my daddy ever did.

Daddy, who was also partial to "Bonaparte's Retreat" and "Pistol Packing Mama," was pretty much tone deaf.

My mother, though, was musically very accomplished. She had a beautiful soprano voice and often soloed at church. I might go to sleep with my daddy singing train songs in a tuneless, drunk, slurring way, but I would wake up to my mother singing Gilbert and Sullivan in the morning. "The flowers that bloom in the spring, tra-la; have nothing to do with your case. For I've come to take under my wing, tra-la; a most unattractive old thing, tra-la; with a caricature for a face. . . . So that's what I mean when I say or I sing; oh, bother the flowers that bloom in the spring."

The bad thing about my family is that there was a lot of violence. My brother and my sisters and I all wrestled and fought, sometimes with disastrous consequences. I have a long scar on my left arm from when my sister Laura and I wrestled each other onto the floor furnace (a metal grid over gas jets) and I scorched my arm. My brother Malcolm once created a rift between my best friend, Eileen Shannon, who lived next door, and me by hitting her over the head with a baseball bat. Once, the five of us were home alone and a fight broke out. During the fight, the kitchen door was slammed to keep Malcolm away. He put up his hands to keep the door from closing, and they crashed through the glass window in the top of the door, carving long hemorrhaging gashes in his arms. I made tourniquets with dish towels, and we called our Aunt Amy, who lived across the street. She took him to the hospital, where my mother and daddy joined them. Malcolm had to have skin grafts from his thighs to repair his arms.

I escaped by spending as much time outside as possible, often up in a tree, or at friends' houses. I spent huge chunks of the day reading and daydreaming. We were encouraged by our parents to read anything we wanted. My mother would tell the library ladies that we were to be allowed in the adult section to pick out books for her. We did, but we also picked out books for ourselves that the authorities had deemed out of our reach. We read all the time: my daddy's union newspaper; my mother's magazines, my friend Eileen's readers from her Catholic school with their tales of girl martyrs who died with beautiful smiles on their faces.

I fell in love with *The New Yorker* and the Algonquin round-table myths. The Algonquin was the New York hotel where the magazine's writers gathered for lunch and conversation that was famously witty and erudite. I read everything I could find by James Thurber and devoured his book *The Years with Ross,* the story of his legendary editor, Harold Ross, at *The New Yorker.* I read all of Robert Benchley's books, too. I fantasized about living surrounded by writers. We also read the *Texas Observer,* the voice of liberal Democrats in the state.

In addition to reading, I sought solace in the church, often going to multiple services on a Sunday. Park Place Methodist Church wasn't an intellectual experience, it was an emotional outlet. At home, my family made fun of me for being emotional, with a quick tendency to burst into tears. At church, you were encouraged to give in to your feelings. My Sunday night fix was the altar call, an emotional invocation from the preacher to come to the Communion rail to rededicate our lives to Christ. Sometimes, if the movement to the front of the church was slow, the congregation would sing repeated choruses of "Love Lifted Me" or "Just As I Am" until the rail filled up. At the end, there were tears and embraces.

As much as I loved the church, I was put off by its emphasis on competition with the nearby Park Place Baptist to see who could build the biggest house of worship. When we finally rebuilt, our preacher erected a sign in front declaring our church: "The Cathedral for the Common Man," offending my mother by its inaccuracy. "You have to have a bishop in residence to be a cathedral," she pointed out. She had been active in the church years before but was appalled by the preacher's pretensions as well as his misuse of the English language.

I also began to be uncomfortable with the racism that surfaced from time to time even in the sanctuary. Racism was as pervasive in the church as it was in the rest of society. Not only were congregations strictly segregated, the preaching also stopped short of tolerance. I once sat through a sermon in my church bemoaning the low birthrate among whites and the rising demographic threat from blacks and Mexican-Americans. I left the church gradually, the result of standard teenaged loathing of what I viewed more and more as its hypocrisy, plus a social life outside the church and a growing distaste for the emotional excess that once so attracted me.

The good things about my family included the constant learning and high expectations. My parents never pointed out anything without calling it by its proper name. It wasn't a pretty bird; it was a cedar waxwing. Those weren't just cattle; they were Black Angus or Herefords or Brahmas. When we drove through the Baytown refinery where my daddy worked, as we often did on Sunday outings, he pointed out the fluid catalytic cracking units and talked about the work being done in the labs, where they were converting petroleum into experimental byproducts, including polystyrene, the now ubiquitous foam in plastic cups and other everyday products.

Other Sunday outings included a tour of the oil super-tanker *Manhattan,* at the time the largest supertanker ever. We also went to see television shows being broadcast and attended an exhibit on nuclear energy, where we learned to imitate the sound of Geiger counters with a staccato gurgle in the back of our throats. And we visited historical sites. The big two in Houston were the San Jacinto Monument, erected on the battlefield where Sam Houston defeated Santa Anna, and the Battleship *Texas,* moored in the San Jacinto River. And, of course, on a family vacation we made that most Texan of pilgrimages, the trip to the Alamo, where I felt I was on hallowed ground.

When I was in second grade, I got promoted a grade up, which put me in the position of being the youngest and often one of the smallest students in my classes. In elementary school, I was academically competitive, especially in the fourth grade, when I was locked in a battle with George Lang, who thought he was smarter than me, to see who could read the most books. But gradually my attention shifted to social life.

By the time I got to high school, I was better groomed. I was a member of the Girl's Booster Club and a Season

Sweetie, part of a chorus line of girls in short cocktail-wait-ress costumes for the big end-of-the year event, the Winter Whirl. I was also one of the four or five smart kids who would be sent over to the educational TV station to inter-view the superintendent of schools. I had a blue-collar chip on my shoulder, my grades (including those in conduct) were frequently bad, and I had a taste for high-school cow-boys. But I scored high on the SATs and picked up a certifi-cate of commendation on the National Merit Scholarship test. I lived a double life, alternating between the usual social life of the high school and my social life with my "intellectual" friends: my best friend, Eric Lueders; my long-time rival, George Lang; and Michael Berryhill. We would head downtown to the Al-Ray Theater to watch Ing-mar Bergman movies and drive around Houston trying to one-up one another about literature, life, or politics.

I had one serious high-school romance, but it ended abruptly. My boyfriend, Jerry Fell, and I had been parked out near the Hobby Airport and left too late to get me home by my curfew. Trying to make up for lost time, Jerry drove way too fast down the Gulf Highway. Apparently there were police cars behind us—the fog was so dense we couldn't see them—and a roadblock ahead designed to stop us. We got off at the neighborhood exit—before we hit the roadblock. The police pulled up behind us and took us downtown. My mother picked me up at the police station. Jerry lost his license, and I was forbidden to see him again.

Most of my high-school classmates didn't go to college. But it was a given in my family that I would. Mother and Daddy had saved enough money to put all five of us through undergraduate school.

In 1963, at age seventeen, I moved to Austin and started school at the University of Texas. Integration was still more a rumor than fact in Texas. Less than half of one percent of the UT student body was black. One evening, crossing the campus to hear a lecture by United Nations assistant secretary and peacemaker Ralph Bunche, I ran into a high-school classmate who had been as racist as they come. He was on his way to the same lecture.

I was surprised, since Bunche was black, and said so.

"Ralph Bunche is a nigger?" he said, and turned on his heels.

It's hard to comprehend how casual and pervasive racial bigotry was back then, how unembarrassed by it people were.

In college I met and became friends with a graduate student who was black. After he left to join the U.S. Army Reserve, he called me frequently. The fact that he was black came up repeatedly in our conversations about our relationship and about his experiences in the Reserve.

During a college break, I went home to Houston and called my closest girlfriend from high school. I had shared daily phone calls with her during high school, spent frequent nights and weekends at her house, and vacationed with her family. We nursed each other through the breakup of various romances and shared with each other what we learned as we fumbled our way toward sex in the backseats of cars.

That's why it hurt so much when she said she couldn't see me.

One of our high-school classmates was in training to be a long-distance operator. She had listened in to a conversation between the graduate student and me. The word was out in the neighborhood: I was dating a black.

I was angry and contemptuous of my friend's refusal to see me. But mostly I was hurt.

It didn't take me long to start flunking out of the University of Texas. At age seventeen, I had been woefully unprepared to live away from home. I was a problem resident in the dorm, depressed and rebellious. They moved me in to room with a slightly older resident whom they viewed as a role model. Karen Couch was a sweet-talking, brown-eyed blond who never offered authorities an argument. She was so outwardly compliant, the dormitory watchdogs never realized that she did exactly what she wanted. Karen spent almost every night with her boyfriend David Danburg at his apartment. The dorm ladies were right: I could learn a lot from Karen.

I moved out of the dormitory illegally, saying that I would be living with my older sister Laura and her husband. Instead, I rented a house with Charmayne Marsh, editor of the campus newspaper, the *Daily Texan*. Not long after, midway through my sophomore year, I was put on scholastic probation and barred from attending classes for a semester. I started dating a United Press International reporter, Bill Hamilton (I called him Hamilton, as did several of his friends). Hamilton covered the state legislature for UPI and frequently traveled to Johnson City to help keep an eye on President Lyndon B. Johnson when he was at his ranch. He also was caught up in the circle of liberal Democrats who partied and politicked throughout Austin at the time. Older than me (twenty-two to my nineteen years), he had been married once and had a two-year-old son, Mark.

Hamilton was a good reporter and a terrific companion. He liked country music as much as I did, and he introduced me to jazz. He had a beautiful stone house just outside of Austin on a ranch that had been a former Civilian Conservation Corps camp. He was ambitious, wanted to travel, and had a gift for the sweet gesture. But still, I had my reservations.

When I found out that I was pregnant, I anticipated breaking up just as soon as the abortion could be taken care of. Hamilton had found a dependable abortionist through a caring general practitioner and had arranged an appointment. Abortions were illegal and often dangerous in 1965.

We traveled to the clinic in Wichita Falls in North Texas on a winter day when there were patches of snow on the ground, speaking very little. The clinic was full of women, many alone and a few with boyfriends. When I walked into the examining room where the abortion would be performed, it looked like any other doctor's office. The only thing out of the ordinary about it was the presence of a black nurse. At the time, a black nurse in a legitimate white doctor's office would have been unthinkable.

I had general anesthesia for the abortion, and when I woke up, Hamilton was there, watching over me and stroking my hair. I thought he was someone I could count on.

When he called me from Acapulco a few months later to propose, I said yes.

I was independent by then. Once I left home, I never went back—staying in Austin and supporting myself during the summer between my freshman and sophomore years and again after my grades forced me out of school.

When Hamilton was transferred to New York, I followed

him a month later. It was a big jump: I was nineteen and had never been out of the South, except for short trips to Mexico. We were married the day after I arrived. My parents had met Hamilton and approved. When I stepped off the plane in New York I was carrying an ivory silk suit from Neiman Marcus and a heavy green coat for the frozen North, gifts from my parents.

I went to work in the library of the *World-Telegram & Sun,* a job that Hamilton helped arrange for me. I had tried and failed to get a job as a copy aide at the *New York Herald-Tribune* because they didn't hire women as copy aides, they said. I was thrilled with myself to be in New York, thrilled to be working at a major newspaper, thrilled to be getting clippings for the newspaper's great columnist Murray Kempton.

I wanted badly to become a reporter, and reporters at the newspaper were generous in referring me to editors at other papers and giving me suggestions about how to find a job. On my days off I would take the train and the bus to suburban newspaper offices, hoping for a chance. One day, I got it. The *Newark News* hired me as a reporter in its Elizabeth bureau. I was elated.

The next day, when I went to work to give notice, the newsroom was in chaos. The *New York Herald-Tribune,* the *New York Journal-American,* and the *World-Telegram & Sun* were merging. Many long-time, talented reporters were losing their jobs. By pure luck, I had mine.

I didn't stay in the job long, but long enough to learn how to do police checks and write obits. Hamilton was offered a job in UPI's Buenos Aires bureau, and we moved just months after I had started work. But I had my credential and my clippings. I was a reporter.

In Buenos Aires, I worked as a stringer and a freelance reporter in a combination of jobs that I found either on my own or with Hamilton's help. I covered a pre–Davis Cup tennis tournament, asking the reporter next to me to explain the strange scoring. I wrote stories about Fulbright students for their hometown newspapers. I did some work as a stringer for *Time* magazine. And I went to Antarctica as a reporter on a cruise arranged by travel entrepreneur Lars Eric Lindblad and did several stories for Copley News Service.

We had been in Argentina about a year when Hamilton decided to give up reporting to take a job in Washington as press secretary to Texas Senator Ralph W. Yarborough. Yarborough was a brilliant liberal Democrat, an early supporter of civil rights and an early opponent of Vietnam. We moved to Washington in the late 1960s, just as civil society in the United States was tearing apart. It was the era of riots and looting, civil-rights triumphs, antiwar demonstrations, and tragedies, including the assassinations of Martin Luther King, Jr., and Bobby Kennedy.

On April 4, 1968, when King was assassinated, fires gutted major retail arteries that served the black communities and looting broke out that night. The fires and the looting continued the next day, and whites fled downtown in their cars. The city was under curfew for six days while the fires and tensions smoldered. Blacks and whites regarded each other with fear and suspicion when they met on the streets of the city.

"Tense, milling crowds of Negroes—angered by the slaying of the Rev. Dr. Martin Luther King—swarmed along 14th street's inner-city strip last night and early today, wrecking and looting stores and heckling policemen," according to the *Post*'s lead story the day after the riots broke out. By the time they were over, there were a dozen dead, including seven who died in fires. Thousands of Washington residents had rioted while thousands of soldiers and National Guardsmen were called in to augment police and firefighters.

When major antiwar protests came to town, Washington had that same city-under-siege feel to it, with Army Reservists stationed on corners with gas masks and fixed bayonets on their rifles. Clouds of tear gas rolled down the street following unauthorized demonstrations against the war. At times, the chaos was so threatening that it seemed as if the United States would fall apart. May Day, a 1971 demonstration that tried and failed to shut down the government, resulted in more than 7,000 arrests.

During the late 1960s and early 1970s I was in Washington most of the time, but I was dividing my time between Washington and Austin, moving down to Texas periodically to work on my college degree. I was still a state resident, entitled to bargain-basement in-state tuition. Hamilton moved back and forth, too, sometimes moving to Austin to work on political campaigns. So we often lived apart.

Although I had always intended to have a career as a reporter, I had also always assumed my career would be secondary to Hamilton's. Now, in part because of the women's movement, I was beginning to believe my career might be just as important.

I worked for awhile for *The Machinist,* the union newspaper I had grown up reading. Usually I was relegated to writing the "Lunchbox" column or captions for "Miss Union Maid," which featured cheesecake photos of union members' wives or daughters, often in bathing suits or other skimpy outfits.

The International Association of Machinists was firmly in favor of the war in Vietnam. Ostensibly on the side of civil rights, some officers of the union thought it was hilarious to call chiggers "chegros." And, like most of the union movement at the time, the Machinists Union was essentially oblivious to discrimination in the workplace. My final story for *The Machinist* was a long feature on the failure of unions to pursue the grievances of women members. It was full of interviews with women activists such as the late Esther Peterson, assistant secretary of labor in the Kennedy administration and director of the President's Commission on the Status of Women. The article was done by the time I left the paper, and the editor assured me it would run. It never did.

I left *The Machinist* to go to work in the Washington bureau of *The New York Journal of Commerce,* a job my former roommate, Charmayne, helped me line up. I covered agriculture, then oil and energy, and briefly, the Supreme Court.

By then, Hamilton had parted ways with Yarborough. It was cold in Washington, and Richard Nixon was president. That seemed to argue for moving to Texas again. We moved, and I drew unemployment until I finally found a job.

I applied to work for a state wildlife magazine, but the editor told me they weren't hiring any women. He wouldn't hire a woman, he said, because the job included trekking around in the West Texas desert. I countered that I had been to the Antarctic. I'd have to spend the night with photographers, and my husband wouldn't like that, he said. It didn't matter what I argued, he wasn't planning to hire a woman.

He was within his legal rights. Congress had left state governments out of the Equal Employment legislation. But I was furious, completely demeaned by the encounter, and determined to strike back. I wrote about it in the *Texas Observer*, hoping it would cost him his job.

I finally found work. Walter Ridder, who worked in the office that Ridder Newspapers' Washington bureau shared with the *Journal of Commerce*, had written me an introduction to economist Walter Rostow, who was teaching at the University of Texas. Rostow referred me to John Gronouski, who had been postmaster general and ambassador to Poland. Gronouski had been hired to be dean of the new Lyndon B. Johnson School of Public Affairs. He hired me as an assistant to help with speeches, a catalogue, and whatever else we needed to cobble together. By default, I also became director of admissions to the graduate school, helping to select the students who would make up the new school's first class.

Meantime, Hamilton and I played tennis, went fishing, shot pool, and attended school full-time. I won an academic scholarship. We organized the antiwar forces in our precinct in Austin and helped push through an antiwar resolution at the state Democratic convention. At first it was great fun, but after awhile life was so easy in Austin, we were beginning to get bored. So when a friend of ours, Jim Hightower, showed up, encouraging us to take jobs in Washington, we were out of there.

Hamilton took a job with the American Federation of State, County and Municipal Employees, and I went to work with Jim at the Agribusiness Accountability Project, a public-interest organization fighting to protect family farmers against corporate agriculture.

Through all my job changes, there was one constant. I seldom worked with or interacted professionally with anyone who was black. It was not atypical that Ralph Yarborough, one of the most progressive liberals in the U.S. Senate, had only a single black employee and no black professionals on staff. Workplace—and cultural and residential—segregation was still very much the rule.

In 1972, when I started to work in the *Post* newsroom, it was the first time I had ever worked side-by-side with black peers. And it was unsettling. We were tense and uneasy around each other. In conversations with black colleagues at the *Post,* I alternated between a gee-whiz-I'm-actually-having-a-conversation-with-a-black kind of incredulity and fear that I would say something wrong. Was it more polite to pretend I didn't notice they were black?

I had decided to return to reporting after about a year at the Agribusiness Accountability Project. I applied to both of the local newspapers, the *Post* and the *Star*. Finally, months after I applied, I heard from the *Post*—on a Sunday afternoon in the summer of 1972. They had just been looking at my resume, a Metro editor said, and it looked interesting. Could I come in and talk to them?

Could I? I was there the next week, not realizing that their sudden interest had been piqued by a discrimination complaint filed by women in the newsroom two months earlier.

Oddly, the thing most of the interviewers seemed focused on was how tough I was. Was I tough enough to be a reporter at the *Washington Post*? I thought I was going to have to hit someone to persuade them to hire me. In the interview with Executive Editor Benjamin C. Bradlee, he asked me what I had been reading. "A book on the Teamsters," I said.

That seemed to be a good answer. They were a tough union.

They decided to offer me the job, in part because City Editor Barry Sussman liked what he saw. Then we launched into salary wrangling. They wanted to hire me, but not if they had to pay a dime more than the small salary I was making in public advocacy.

"I'm not saying, 'Take it, or leave it,'" said Metro editor Harry Rosenfeld. "I'm saying, 'Please, take it,'" he said.

"Or leave it?" I asked.

"That's right," said Rosenfeld.

I took it.

How could I say no to what I viewed as the best newspaper in the country?

Warren's Story

New Orleans was never the "Big Easy" for people of color, unless your color allowed you to pass for white. But success in that endeavor came with dangers. Genes could betray. What looked white one day could be born black or brown the next. That meant trouble for people who sneaked across the color line.

No one wanted that kind of trouble in a place that expressly forbade miscegenation, the interbreeding of presumably distinct human races. But what was outlawed by day was practiced with vigor at night.

New Orleans was thus a community of lies in matters of race. The whole State of Louisiana was a racial lie shared by blacks and whites alike.

Blacks frequently hid the whites on their family trees, largely out of shame. Interracial sex during slavery, the

Reconstruction Era, and the Jim Crow years was mostly a one-way street, with white men taking advantage of black women.

Whites also hid their racial skeletons. A white family named Avery might live across the street from a black family named Avery. But custom and segregation laws kept them apart.

My childhood and much of my adulthood were shaped by racial lies and contradictions. I used to pretend that wasn't the case. There was comfort in self-delusion. But the truth is that race touched and defined nearly everything about me.

My parents, Daniel Thomas Brown, Sr., and Lillian Gadison Provost-Brown, tried mightily to protect me and my brothers and sisters from the evils of racism. They relied on education and the Catholic Church for defense. They also formed loose alliances with southern Jews, who offered us weekend jobs and, later, scholarships.

But racism in Louisiana was as pervasive as the miasma that rose from its swamps and bayous. It got into everything.

I remember the first time I paid attention to the word "nigger." That's the first time I paid attention to it, but not the first time I heard it.

"Nigger" was white noise in black New Orleans life. It was

the ugly background music of our existence. You heard it, but ignored it; or you pretended that you didn't hear it at all.

But, sometimes, the word came through with stunning clarity. I must have been about nine years old when it happened. That would have been in 1957. I'm judging from the arrival of the Murray bicycles. There were four children in the Brown household then—my two older brothers, Danny and Bobby, me, and our little sister DaLinda.

Daddy bought the blue Murray bike, the one without the crossbar, for DaLinda. But she was too small to ride it. So my brothers assigned it to me, the youngest and smallest of the boys. The bigger Murray, the red one with the crossbar, went to Danny and Bobby.

Bobby and I were riding the bikes on North Galvez Street in the city's predominantly black Ninth Ward when two white policemen stopped us. They were riding in a patrol car. They flashed their lights and wailed their siren and pulled us over.

"Where'd you little niggers get those bikes?" one of the policemen asked.

"Our daddy gave us these bikes!" I shouted back, ignoring the reference to us as "niggers." My brother Bobby had the bigger body, but I had the biggest mouth.

"Then your nigger daddy musta' stole those bikes," the policeman said.

Our daddy was a respected science teacher in the city's black public high schools. He had a master's degree in biology from Xavier University of Louisiana, the only black Catholic college in the United States. Blacks either called him Mr. Brown or "Professor Dan." Nobody called him "nigger."

Bobby put a hand on my shoulder in a failed attempt to restrain my tongue.

"Our daddy isn't a thief and he isn't a nigger," I yelled at the policeman. He turned red. We turned scared.

"Ain't that somethin'?" the other policeman asked his partner. "You hear that little nigger? 'Our daddy isn't... Our daddy isn't....'" I suppose those rednecks expected me to say "ain't."

The policemen found my use of correct grammar funny. They laughed at us, got in their patrol car, and drove away.

We told Daddy about the encounter. He was succinct in response. The policemen were wrong, Daddy said. But they had guns and uniforms. All we had were bikes.

"I could always get you more bikes," he said. "But I can't get you another life. The next time, Warren, learn to keep your mouth shut."

I didn't learn.

Our church was Holy Redeemer, located between Esplanade Boulevard and Elysian Fields Avenue a short distance from the city's French Quarter. Holy Redeemer was

———

one of three popular black Catholic churches in New Orleans when I was growing up. The other two with large congregations were Corpus Christi in the city's Seventh Ward (the black "Creole Belt") and St. Peter Claver near the destitute, crime-ridden Desire Housing Projects in the Ninth Ward. Our parents forbade us to go anywhere near the Desire projects.

On Sundays when we didn't have time to get to Mass at Holy Redeemer or Corpus Christi, which required traveling by bus, my two brothers and I would walk to the white St. Mary's Catholic Church near our home.

New Orleans was like that. Blacks and whites who weren't rich tended to live near one another, though they might as well have been oceans apart in terms of local practice and custom.

St. Mary's, like other white Catholic churches in the city, allowed blacks to attend Mass as long as they sat in separate sections or stood in the rear of the church and waited for whites to receive Holy Communion first. Even as an eleven-year-old, the year of my second biggest mouth opening, I found this ridiculous.

On one of those St. Mary's Sundays, I walked up to the Communion rail ahead of the white communicants. The priest and altar boy serving Communion ignored me. They served all of the whites first. Then, they came back to me.

———

"Body of Christ," the priest said, lifting the host in front of my face.

"No, thank you," I said, and walked away.

I didn't notice the faces of any of the white congregation, and I didn't look behind me to see what the priest was doing or saying after my protest. But I saw the face of my oldest brother, Danny, when I returned to the back of the church. He was mad! He knocked me in the back of the head.

"Are you stupid?" Danny asked. "You're going to get us in trouble...."

Danny couldn't wait to tell Daddy about my behavior. Daddy was pissed, too.

"I send you to Mass, and you try to go to jail?" he asked in a tone similar to Danny's. "Are you stupid?"

"You could've all gotten into trouble. You could've gotten yourself and your brothers killed or arrested. What if someone knew you were my son? I could lose my job. You're man enough to pull a stunt like that? Are you man enough to feed this family?"

I was simultaneously devastated, scared, and angry. I wanted to say something smart-assed to Daddy. But he was right. I wasn't man enough to feed the family.

Daddy and Mommie (we pronounced it Momm-mee, with the accent on the "mee") slept in a bedroom in the front of our house on Clouet Street. The girl's bedroom, for DaLinda and new baby sister Loretta Marie at that time, was next to our parents' bedroom. The boys' bedroom was in the back of the house, behind the bathroom and next to the kitchen. Voices had a way of drifting through the house, especially at night when everyone was supposed to be asleep.

"I don't know what we're going to do about that boy and his mouth," I heard my father saying to my mother.

"He just talks too damned much," said my mother, a sweet woman, more Catholic than the Pope, but who could curse a blue streak when she got the notion.

"He has a talent for opening his mouth to get into trouble. I just hope he learns how to use it to get out," my father said.

I didn't learn.

I loved words. I could read well and fast at an early age. I can't remember when I couldn't read; my parents indulged me and my siblings, who also were readers, by buying lots of books, newspapers, and magazines.

When I was in the eighth grade at Holy Redeemer, in 1961, there was a story in the *Times-Picayune,* the city's leading white newspaper, about a man who was killed by his wife at a girlfriend's home, where the wife found him "camped" in the girlfriend's "diggings." That sounded pretty interesting. The story went on to say that the man was a "bigamist." What the hell was that?

My father brought lots of dictionaries home from the high schools where he taught. He also had connections at the New Orleans Public School Board, which he used to get access to the better dictionaries and books given to white public-school students. The black kids were using the older and more abbreviated *Thorndike* dictionaries. The white kids got *Webster's*. I looked up "bigamist" in Webster's and got what I thought was a great idea.

The Missionary Sisters Servants of the Holy Ghost at Holy Redeemer, many of whom came from Ireland, wore gold wedding bands. But none of them had husbands. I asked Sister Irene, the school's principal, why she wore a wedding ring.

"Because I'm a bride of Christ," she said piously.

This was too good to be true.

"What about Sister Vincent?" I asked.

"She's a bride of Christ, too," said Sister Irene.

Hmmm.

"And Sister Mary Frances?" I inquired.

"We're all brides of Christ, Warren!" replied an exasperated Sister Irene.

My moment had come.

"Is Christ a bigamist?" I asked.

Sister Irene turned crimson. Slap! I felt the sting. She sent me to detention. She called the parish priest. The priest called my father. Daddy was not happy.

Nevertheless, I got into St. Augustine High School the following fall. This was a very big deal. St. Augustine, founded in 1951 by the fathers of the Society of St. Joseph, was (and remains) the top black Catholic high school for males in the South. More than 90 percent of its graduates go to college; and the majority of those who get into college complete undergraduate work and go on to earn postgraduate degrees.

Black Catholic families in New Orleans made enormous financial and other sacrifices to get their boys into St. Augustine. My parents were no different. They sent Bobby and me to St. Augustine. Danny, who could never accept the idea of attending an all-boys' anything, attended Xavier University Preparatory, when that school was still accepting male students.

Black Catholic girls went to St. Mary's Academy and Xavier Prep. All three of my sisters, including the last-born, Mary Edith, went to Xavier Prep.

St. Augustine, home of the "Purple Knights," was tough. I spent my entire eighth-grade year agonizing over whether I would pass the admissions test to get in and wondering if I would wind up in the A, B, C, or D class if admitted. Top students were placed in the A class. Those with lower test scores were assigned to B class, and so on.

My verbal skills got me into the B class. My mathematical ineptitude kept me there for my entire academic career at St. Augustine. Bobby tested into the A class and stayed there for four years, which always was something of a mystery to me, because he never studied for anything.

Integration, or what passed for it in New Orleans, came while we were at St. Augustine. Even the Catholic Church decided that it was time for the "Mystical Body of Christ" to include blacks and whites together. But the city's Catholic whites didn't want to hear it. They didn't even want black and white Catholic students to compete against one another in sports. Athletic seasons would end with "black Catholic high-school city champions" and "white Catholic high-school city champions," the latter of whom were regarded by the local media as the "real" champions.

That angered St. Augustine students and faculty. It angered the city's black community, Catholics and Protestants alike. At stake was more than athletic pride. The white champions got scholarships to big-name colleges. The black champions didn't.

Father Robert Grant, white, our school principal, fought hard to get rid of that segregated system. He was assisted in that endeavor by Father Joseph Verrett, black, the school's vice principal.

The issue came to a head in 1965 when both St. Augustine and the white Catholic Jesuit High School finished their basketball seasons with perfect records. Jesuit got the "city champion" headlines. St. Augustine got the footnote.

In a dramatic development, captured in the 1999 fictionalized TNT original movie, *Passing Glory*, Fathers Grant and Verrett, assisted by legions of others, arranged a "closed-door game" on February 26, 1965, between St. Augustine and Jesuit. St. Augustine won. Subsequently, Father Grant succeeded in a federal lawsuit to integrate the exclusively white Louisiana High School Athletic Association, allowing St. Augustine to compete against white schools in all sports.

That was a good development in more ways than one. There was the myth of the physically superior (and mentally inferior) black male. A number of my black friends and classmates grew up believing that myth, too. Whites might be smart, they thought, but blacks could kick white ass in anything physical.

But I never accepted that thinking. My scrawny little body was too much of a contradiction to validate the Mandango fantasy. White girls could have slapped me silly, and I would not have had the physical wherewithal to do anything about it. That is why I relied on words to make an impression.

Interracial athletic competition eventually laid that myth to rest in New Orleans. White boys could jump. St. Augustine did not always beat Jesuit on the basketball court. Jesuit did not routinely beat St. Augustine on Scholastic Aptitude Tests.

There was little question about where I would attend college. Ours was a "Xavier family." Our father had earned his degrees from there. Our mother had worked there for decades as a switchboard operator. Our mother's employment assured us full scholarships, as long as we maintained a "B" academic average.

I didn't.

I joined a fraternity, Alpha Phi Omega. I joined the school newspaper, *The Xavier Herald*. I spent more time with the fraternity and in the newspaper's office than I did in the classroom. I finished with a 1.7 grade point average at the end of my first year.

Xavier should've kicked me out. But out of deference to my parents, the school's administration gave me a second chance. Daddy gave me the same options he had earlier given to Danny: "Improve your grade point average, or improve your marksmanship. It's either Xavier or the U.S. Army, son. You choose."

Danny chose the Army. Daddy accompanied him to the recruiting station.

Some of my neighborhood friends and high-school classmates who weren't fortunate enough to get into college were dying in Vietnam. Some of them died before I finished my first freshman semester at Xavier. I decided to study; but I didn't give up my forum at the *Herald*, where I became an associate editor.

There is nothing like walking on campus in the morning when everyone is reading your column, especially during a period of turmoil. Along with Vietnam, there was the Black Power movement, a more activist and frequently more violent version of the civil-rights campaign.

I supported the U.S. war in Vietnam, which was easy to do from the safety of my campus newspaper office. I opposed the Black Power movement, which was a hell of a lot more difficult to do on a black campus.

My opposition to the Black Power movement, as it manifested itself in New Orleans in the late 1960s, was based on my opposition to hatred. Killing "whitey" was never an option in our family. "Those whom the gods would destroy, they first make angry," Daddy always warned. He and my mother insisted that the battle could be won in the classroom, which is why I adamantly opposed militants' attempts to shut down the university every time they

wanted to make a point to Xavier's "Uncle Tom administration."

That time on campus was an ironic period for me. New
Orleans was and remains a very color conscious town.
Light-skinned blacks routinely shunned darker blacks.
"Light, bright, and near-damned-white" blacks often felt a
sense of entitlement. Being of darker hue, I was on the
receiving end of much of their stupidity throughout my
elementary and high-school years, and during my freshman
year at Xavier.

But a strange thing happened as the Black Power movement moved forward. Light-skinned blacks, who once valued long, silky hair, began wearing Afros. Although they
had once shunned me because I was darker, they now
avoided me because I was "a running dog lackey of the
white establishment." They were revolutionaries. I was a
counterrevolutionary. It was all deliciously entertaining. We
fought one another until we graduated and went on to earn
other degrees or to take jobs in the white establishment.

I graduated from Xavier in 1969, the same year I married
Mary Anne. I always had an eye for pretty women, and
Mary Anne was one of the prettiest women in Xavier University's freshman class of 1966. She was a little thing, obvi-
ously a small-town girl, as evidenced by her tendency to
wear black bobby socks with white tennis shoes and shift

dresses. No sister from big-city New Orleans would wear an outfit like that, and Mary Anne surely enough was a sister, even though she looked like she could have been Hispanic, or Asian, or the progeny of a variety of other ethnic groups.

In that regard, she blended well with New Orleans' black community, where the terms "colored" and "Negro" and "black" were more terms of art than anything else. "Black" included people who looked whiter than the whitest white and darker than the darkest black and a whole palette of colors in between. The only thing that mattered was whether you had some black blood somewhere in your family, and Mary Anne's multiracial family certainly had a lot of that.

"Black blood" made you black no matter how much "white blood" was circulating through your veins—a Deep South standard for ethnicity that made me secretly proud. Just the tiniest bit of black blood "turned" you black. Damn, I thought, black blood is some powerful stuff.

Anyway, I followed Mary Anne around campus for several weeks, always looking for an excuse to stop to talk to her. I was a sophomore and a member of Alpha Phi Omega fraternity. I figured she'd be impressed with those credentials. She wasn't. Instead, during one of my stalking episodes, she asked: "Why are you following me around?" I lied—told her that I had better things to do than to keep tabs on a first-year woman, especially inasmuch as there were a whole bunch of sophomore, junior, and senior women to look at. She scoffed and walked away.

But I had her attention, and I built on that connection at the university's daily Mass. Mary Anne attended Mass at every opportunity in her college days, which turned out to be a good thing for me. I was a Xavier acolyte, and I served nearly every Mass she attended, which means I also assisted in serving her Holy Communion. In those days, the acolyte held a thin platter under the chin of the person receiving Communion. That was to prevent any elements of the Communion from falling to the floor.

I always made sure to hold the platter close to Mary Anne's chin as the priest was giving her Holy Communion. She'd close her eyes, lift her head, stick out her tongue—and I would melt. The woman had the prettiest tongue. Mea culpa, mea culpa, mea maxima culpa. Sometimes, she'd open her eyes as she was receiving the wafer, and I'd look at her and smile. She wouldn't smile back. But I could be sure that she'd catch up with me after Mass to lecture me on my sacrilegious behavior.

What the hell? Whatever worked, like when I saw her on the floor at a university dance trying to get some silly freshman dude to do some steps. The brother couldn't dance. I could. I danced with her all night long.

———

41

We courted for three years, including a year of engage-
ment. I promised her that we'd marry as soon as I got my
bachelor's degree, because there was no way I was going to
marry anybody without that degree and a job to go along
with it. I got the degree and the job, becoming a news clerk
on the National Desk of the *New York Times* after abandon-
ing an internship at *Newsday* in Garden City, Long Island. I
also got a *New York Times* scholarship to pursue a master's
degree in journalism at Columbia University. Mary Anne
and I married on August 23, 1969.

The *Times* was an eye-opener. I worked for the irascible
Irv Horowitz, whose idea of teaching was to make the student suffer as much as possible. I suffered, and I learned. Irv
wasn't about black or white. He was about getting things
done correctly. He once told me to track down Jim Wooten,
a journalist who was then in the *Times* Atlanta bureau. I
called Wooten's house several times and couldn't get him. I
made the mistake of telling Irv that Wooten wasn't home.

"How the hell do you know that?" Irv thundered back.
"Are you in Atlanta? Can you see into his house? How the
hell do you know he's not at home? All you know is that he
didn't answer the phone. That's all you're supposed to say.
Never again tell me or anyone else around here what you
don't know."

I got the point. I also got good guidance from several

black reporters who were on the *Times* staff. They taught me how to choose my battles. They also taught me when to retreat. "You don't want to hang around here after you finish Columbia," said Tom Johnson, the first black reporter on a major newspaper to serve as a foreign correspondent.

"You came here as a news clerk," Johnson said. "They will always see you as a news clerk, with or without your Columbia degree. Get out of here. Go to a smaller newspaper. Work your way back."

I returned to New Orleans, where I became the first full-time black reporter on the now-defunct *New Orleans States-Item,* the afternoon version of the *Times-Picayune.* Both were owned by Newhouse Newspapers, Inc.

"Can you type?" Seriously, that was the first thing a *States-Item* editor asked me.

I belonged to the mod squad at the *States-Item.* It consisted of me and two white reporters, Danny Greene and Christopher Shearhouse. The newspaper considered them hippies. I regarded them as friends. For a long time, they were the only whites who would work with me in the *States-Item* newsroom.

We covered lots of stories together, including a daylong shoot-out between the New Orleans police and the Black Panther Party in the Desire Housing Projects. Danny almost got us killed in that one. We were caught by some

Black Panther supporters who thought we were cops. Danny offered to show them our press cards. I panicked. New Orleans press cards back then were emblazoned with the seal of the New Orleans Police Department. Before I could stop Danny, he flashed the card, and the Panther sympathizers stuck guns in our faces. We made the front page with a first-person story.

Robert DeLeon, the young black journalist who had recruited me for *Newsday,* had moved on to Johnson Publishing Company in Chicago, where he was serving as managing editor of the "Black bible," *Jet* magazine, the nation's leading black newsweekly.

The year was 1971. "I'll double your salary if you leave those honkies and work for me," DeLeon said. It was an offer I could not refuse. I went to Chicago—but didn't stay long. *Jet* more appropriately can be compared to the *National Enquirer* than *Time* or *Newsweek*. It gives the basic news. But it's mostly about movie stars, athletes, relationship counseling, and gossip. I wanted to be a reporter. I went to the *Philadelphia Inquirer* at the invitation of Gene Roberts, who was in charge of the National Desk when I worked at the *New York Times.* Roberts was straightforward. "I don't consider *Jet* journalism," he said. "As far as I'm concerned, you've wasted a year. Come to the *Inquirer,* start over, work a year as a police reporter. If you do well, I'll send you to the state capitol bureau."

By the time I arrived in Philadelphia in 1972, a number of blacks already were on the newspaper's staff. Chief among them was Acel Moore, a veteran reporter who gave me some more good advice: "Know more about your beat than anyone else. Know as much about other peoples' beats as they do. Write your ass off."

It worked. And Roberts kept his word, too. Within a year after I'd arrived at the *Inquirer,* the paper moved me to its state capitol bureau in Harrisburg, where, once again, I became the "only black" in the newsroom. But I was fortunate enough to work under a great editor and equally good person, Bill Eccenbarger. He was a white Pennsylvanian. But I seldom thought of him in terms of color, because he never dealt with me that way. We became friends and colleagues.

Harrisburg also offered me Herbert Denenberg, who was then Pennsylvania's insurance commissioner, and later a member of the state's Public Utilities Commission. Denenberg was a consumer advocate, a man in the Don Quixote mode. He loved taking on big companies and beating them with statistics. He collared me one day in the Capitol building.

"What do you think is the biggest taxing authority in the state?" Denenberg asked.

"The legislature," I said.

"Wrong," Denenberg said. "Every time the PUC allows a rate increase, it's effectively raising taxes. That's big news, but none of you people in the newsroom understand it. How would you like to understand it? How would you like to get on page one every other week?"

That sounded good to me. I became Denenberg's devoted student. I got on page one of the *Philadelphia Inquirer* every other week. Sometimes, I got on every day of the week. Denenberg was my hero. So were Judy Bachrach and Karlyn Barker, two white Columbia classmates who were working at the *Washington Post*. They recommended me to Elsie Carper.

The *Post* was on the hunt for "qualified" blacks and other minorities, and Elsie was assigned to lead the effort. The paper also was on the lookout for more "qualified" women, which meant white women, because "blacks and minorities" also included black and other minority women, in the racial shorthand of the time.

Bachrach and Barker recommended me to the *Post*'s editors. I was doing well at the *Inquirer*. I went to the *Post*'s interviews feeling quite arrogant. Maybe that's what it took to get hired at the newspaper in those days of executive editor Ben Bradlee's rule.

After a day of being grilled by a series of *Post* editors, I wound up in Bradlee's office.

"What do you think about our racial situation at the *Post*?" Bradlee asked.

"I don't give a damn about your racial situation at the *Post*," I said. "I'm here because I thought you wanted to hire a good reporter."

Bradlee could barely control his contempt for my response.

"What do you call a good reporter?" he asked.

"You're the one who's doing the hiring. What do you call a good reporter?" I countered.

"Somebody who doesn't watch the goddamned clock to see when it's time to leave. Somebody who knows how to go after a story. Somebody who's got balls," Bradlee said.

"Fine," I said. "If you hire me, you've got a good reporter. If that helps your racial situation, that's your business."

My big mouth, again. I didn't care. Bradlee couldn't fire me from the *Inquirer,* after all. I figured I'd never get hired at the *Post* after that performance in his office.

Harry Rosenfeld, the *Post*'s national editor at the time, caught me as I was leaving the newsroom. He looked as if he had just had a hard laugh.

"Where are you going?" Rosenfeld asked. "You got the job."

[2]

The 1970s

Falling Apart, Coming Together

We came to the *Post* in the middle of a revolution.

In the 1970s, the nation was in turmoil. Americans were still stunned by the assassinations of the 1960s—John F. Kennedy, Martin Luther King, Jr., and Robert F. Kennedy. Race riots had torn through major cities. A war was raging on the streets and campuses over U.S. involvement in Vietnam. In Washington, armed National Guard troops often were posted on the corners to monitor antiwar protests, which continued. At Kent State University in Ohio, government troops fired on and killed unarmed students. And there was Watergate, the political scandal uncovered by two young *Washington Post* reporters, Bob Woodward and Carl Bernstein. Watergate rocked the nation and drove President Nixon from office.

It was a period of violent and nonviolent transformation, and newspapers were changing, too. The *Post* was in the lead in changing the way journalism was practiced. In the newsroom there was an aura of excitement and an incredible sense of potential. The *Post* had demonstrated enormous courage publishing the Pentagon Papers and pursuing Watergate despite powerful opposition.

The *Post* also was a leader in creating the "new journalism," a livelier, more personal approach; practitioners at the paper included Tom Wolfe and Nicholas von Hoffman. Editor Larry Stern had replaced the traditional women's section with "Style," a new forum for cultural and social commentary and reporting on trends. "Style" had style. It was sassy, irreverent, inventive. It took off the white gloves.

The *Post* was the place to be, and we thought we were lucky to be there. But it wasn't just luck, or just a combination of luck and talent. Newspapers had been bastions of white male expression. Now, they were being forced to reflect the realities and sentiments of the larger society.

The Kerner Commission, created by President Lyndon B. Johnson to study the causes of the 1960s riots, took the segregated news media to task for failing to cover black Americans and acting "as if Negroes do not read newspapers or watch television, give birth, marry, die or go to PTA meetings." It also indicted the press for failing to communicate to "both their black and white audiences a sense of the problems America faces and the sources of potential solutions."

Watergate established the *Post* as a giant-killer in journalism, and it also resulted in a wave of hiring at the newspaper. Many of the new reporters making their way into the newsroom weren't far removed from college campuses where activism was the order of the day. They might have left their protest signs on campus when they joined the *Post*, but they remained captured by the spirit of the times.

Sometimes the activism was transformed into aggressive investigative reporting. The *Washington Post* had a strong history of muckraking even before Watergate. It had always attracted reporters such as Morton Mintz who wanted to use their craft to right wrongs, and now it was an even stronger magnet for those journalists.

Some of that passion was turned toward knocking down barriers at the *Washington Post* itself. A group of black reporters who became known as the Metro Seven filed a complaint with the Equal Employment Opportunity Commission in 1972 over the newspaper's inadequate coverage of the black community and discrimination against minority employees. The Metro Seven were LaBarbara

Bowman, Ivan Brandon, Leon Dash, Mike Hodge, Penny Mickelbury, Richard Prince, and Ron Taylor. Clifford Alexander, who would later become secretary of the army, was their attorney.

Less than a month later, women in the *Post* newsroom filed their own complaint protesting the newspaper's failure to hire and promote women. "We were just having trouble getting them in the door," said Karlyn Barker, one of the participants. When the *Post* failed to respond adequately, they filed a class-action complaint (in which some of their male colleagues participated) with the EEOC on May 29, 1972. The complaint was settled in 1980 with a token back pay award and commitments by the *Post* to do more to hire and promote women.

Without those efforts to bring more blacks and women into the newsroom, the two of us might never have been hired by the *Washington Post*. We might never have worked together or become friends. We might never have wound up on operating tables in adjoining rooms.

Slowly, the *Washington Post* began hiring more blacks and women. But the newspaper made beginner's errors in diversity. It frequently grabbed the wrong people and fumbled when it found the right ones.

Affirmative action required a refinement that the *Post* simply did not have. The newspaper that once kept blacks and women out by looking at them as blacks and women, instead of as individuals with varying degrees of talent, now allowed them in just because they were blacks and women. The management had been so good at discriminating against blacks and women that at first it had a hard time discriminating among them. The paper hired blacks who couldn't decide whether they were reporters or political activists first, and it took on women who had never practiced daily journalism. It wound up hiring people who could talk a good line, but couldn't write one.

Some of the people coming in to the newsroom had been stars in smaller galaxies, but they flamed out in the new, intensely competitive universe of the *Post*.

And the *Post* wasn't any different from the rest of the newspaper world or most of the major institutions in America. The jobs at the top belonged to white men who reached out for reporters who reminded them of themselves at the same age—young white guys. They could identify with young white guys, and it was difficult for them to relate to us.

Even for white men, the *Post* often wasn't a welcoming environment. Ben Bradlee was a great editor who created a very competitive workplace. But he was a social Darwinist editor who put Martin Luther King, Jr.'s, "creative tension" to new uses in the newsroom.

The main newsroom, even then, was huge, full of hundreds of desks. The *Post* had moved into a new building in the early 1970s, and the décor was more corporate office than old-fashioned newsroom. And off the main newsroom there were satellite sections—Sports, Style, and Business. Friendships were often determined by proximity. If you didn't work in the same section with someone, you might go years without meeting. For the first several years we worked at the *Post,* we barely knew each other. Martha knew who Warren was because there were so few blacks in the newsroom that they stood out. Warren didn't have a clue who Martha was—just another white woman on the Metro staff where most of the women who weren't in Style were concentrated.

But Warren did know every black in the newsroom. Because they were in the minority, black reporters, editors, news researchers, and copy aides tended to band together. They also reached out to blacks in other parts of the newspaper, including custodial staff, who were often treated as non-persons by many *Post* editors and reporters.

The *Post* didn't have the kind of after-hours collegiality that was the norm at many other newspapers. There wasn't any mentoring or career guidance. For reporters who weren't accustomed to being ignored or not having a patron, the *Post* could be a lonely and confusing place. A mistake in a story or a development misread could make you feel even more isolated, or as if you were bleeding in the water and attracting the sharks.

Both of us made friends and had good relations with our colleagues. But we often felt out of place. We felt like we were admitted to the club, but we didn't know the rules. Many of our colleagues came from Ivy League schools and well-to-do families and brought with them a sense of entitlement. We felt talented but not entitled.

Warren often felt like a reluctantly invited guest at a dinner party where everyone was watching to see if he knew which fork to use. Martha watched white male colleagues slip into easy familiarity with the man they called "Ben," while she was suppressing the instinct to call him "Mr. Bradlee." We felt like public defenders in a room full of corporate lawyers. We knew we were their equals, but we had the sneaking suspicion they didn't see us that way. We hadn't been to Ivy League undergraduate schools. (Neither had Leonard Downie, Jr., now executive editor of the *Washington Post,* who in the 1970s was jokingly called "Land-grant Len" because he had attended a land-grant college, Ohio State.) We didn't sound like William Buckley. We didn't have ambassadors as family or family friends. We'd never been to the Hamptons.

Of course, neither of us shared these feelings with each

other or anyone else. We didn't want to show our vulnerability.

Meanwhile, the city served by the *Washington Post* was changing fundamentally. Race relations in Washington were still uneasy in the wake of the riots. Socially and economically, it was really two cities with long burned-out scars reminding everyone of the deepness of the division.

Political control of the majority black city was in the hands of congressional committees dominated by reactionary southern Democrats, who ruled because of a seniority system on Capitol Hill that was beginning to crumble. And economic control of the city was in the hands of the white, male-dominated business community. The city had a presidentially appointed black mayor, Walter Washington, and an appointed city council that had little power.

The city's civic leadership and civil-rights activists were pressing Congress to grant Washingtonians the right to elect a mayor and city council and to control their own finances. There also was a move to give the city voting rights in Congress. Washington residents had gained the right to vote in presidential elections in the early 1960s, when the Twenty-third Amendment was adopted. Now the issue was home rule.

Martha's beat covered the area's congressional delegation, which meant she followed the emotionally charged fight for home rule. Black activists in D.C. chafed over the lack of control, charging that the city was being run like a plantation. Many older whites were filled with fear over putting the city's fate in the hands of the majority. And many members of Congress who had enjoyed wielding control over the city were reluctant to give up their powers.

In the course of that coverage, she made friends with Colbert I. King, now the deputy editorial page editor of the *Washington Post*. At the time, Colby was the minority counsel to the Senate District Committee working for Republican Senator Charles McC. Mathias. Mathias was a supporter of greater rights for D.C. residents and helped craft the home-rule legislation.

Mathias was part of a larger coalition of blacks and whites, Democrats and Republicans, who prevailed on the issue. One of the most important players was Walter Washington, often reviled by more outwardly activist blacks as an "Uncle Tom." Although he sometimes didn't get enough credit for it, Washington was a skillful politician, as forceful behind the scenes as he was nonthreatening to whites in public.

Through Colby, who is black and who had grown up in D.C. and attended the city's academically prestigious Dunbar High School, Martha began to develop a greater appreciation of the city as a hometown. Colby, and his wife, Gwen, also opened her eyes in another way. The first time Martha went to a dinner party at their home, she and Hamilton were in a minority among the black guests. Initially, having always been a member of the dominant culture, it felt strange to be in the minority. But after a minute or two, Martha shrugged. "So this is what it's like," she thought, realizing that Colby and other blacks who moved in mostly white professional circles must often find themselves in similar situations.

Outside the political arena, Washington was still a small town and not a very interesting one. The restaurants were either clubby or crummy. It was hard to get a decent meal after 8 P.M. The dress style was dowdy. Except for the black-white racial divide, there was little diversity in the Washington metropolitan area or in its economy, which depended on the federal government.

The *Post* itself was shaken in the 1970s—by a divisive strike by the press operators. Some reporters and editors worked during the strike; others honored the picket lines. Martha supported the press operators' strike, forming the Rank and File Strike Support Committee with colleagues Elizabeth Becker and John Hanrahan. Even after the strike ended in 1976, the bitterness lingered.

Warren was hired in the aftermath of the strike. He walked into an unhappy home. The tension was palpable in the very divided newsroom. Some people still weren't speaking. A newcomer, unaware of the grievances, could unwittingly draw fire by being perceived to support one side or the other.

Both of us went through highs and lows during our early careers at the *Post*. Both of us had our preening moments, when everyone was talking about the stories we had done. But both of us also went through periods when nobody remembered our names. By the end of the 1970s, we were drifting professionally.

That's when Frank Swoboda grabbed us. Frank hired both of us as reporters in the Business section. It was a typical Frank move. He has a way of getting the best out of bad situations and of getting the best out of people. He's also a world-class snoop who literally knew everything going on in the newsroom. Frank knew that neither of us was happy where we were. He figured that undervalued people had a need to prove themselves. He was right.

Frank was in charge of the Business section from 1982 to 1987. A former wire-service reporter who had covered the White House, he was working in the Washington bureau of the *Baltimore Sun* when his predecessor, Peter Silberman, sought him out and hired him for the *Post* in 1978. When Pete left to take over the National staff, Frank took over the Business section.

———

He created the only section in the newsroom where a sense of humor was required for admission. Even deadline tension was different in Frank's section. Other editors might show irritation with reporters who were slow to turn in stories. Frank would stand over you and chant: "Faster, faster ... "

He didn't destroy egos. He built them. As soon as both of us came on staff, he assigned us stories that were candidates for the front page. It was a vote of confidence that prompted us to do our best work. We didn't want to let ourselves down. We didn't want to let Frank down. We got on the front page regularly, often beating the competition by having the story first, or reporting it better.

Frank continued the work that Silberman had begun— building the Business section and making it more professional. In the process, he attracted other reporters and editors who were dedicated to the mission and who, more importantly, knew how to have fun. The hallmark of the *Post* newsroom was self-importance. What Frank created was a place where reporters and editors took their work very seriously, but not themselves.

When columnist Mary McGrory arrived at the *Post* from the competing *Washington Star* after it folded in 1981, she was struck by how people were so absorbed, either in work or themselves, at 9:30 or 10 in the morning that they couldn't look up to say "good morning." She also was struck, she said, by the fact that when she heard laughter, it was always coming from the Business section.

Any event was an excuse for a cake. We had cakes for birthdays, news scoops, arriving and departing staffers, or just because we were hungry. We had cakes when the Dow went up, and we had cakes when the Dow went down.

We had games and toys. We practiced "gotchas," elaborate practical jokes carried off with cooperation and precision by the whole staff. Frank was particularly good at sniffing out "gotchas," so overcoming his sharply honed defenses was an irresistible challenge.

One day, as deadline approached, one by one, every reporter on the financial staff came to Frank with plausible potential front-page stories, more major stories than the section had ever handled. If it had been true, Frank would have been there all night making sure they were edited right, that they had art, and that there were enough columns of news space. It was only when he headed toward the managing editor's office to deliver the news that two members of the staff shouted "Gotcha!"

Even with an editor as wonderful as Frank, blacks and women in the Business section were still struggling to be treated the same as white male reporters. Once, when the secretary of the treasury was invited to lunch at the *Post* by the Business section, no blacks or women were included at the event, triggering a protest. Usually, top reporters and editors were invited to these lunches, small gatherings in a wood-paneled boardroom upstairs. And there were black reporters and women reporters on the financial staff who should have been included and who would have benefited from the opportunity. Frank never made that mistake again.

Women on the staff also had to persuade Frank, an old-school guy, that not only was it "socially acceptable" to go to lunch with women reporters, and not a sign of a sexual dalliance, it was also necessary for their career advancement.

Frank carried some of the same assumptions and prejudices into the newsroom that other white male editors did. What made Frank different was his inherent sense of fair play and his openness to suggestions that the playing field wasn't level.

You could raise those issues without fear of reprisal. More than that, with Frank, you could raise them with an expectation that he would understand and that something positive would result.

Frank evolved. He named Martha as the first woman editor on the financial assignment desk. Because he was Frank, he did it with self-effacing jokes about appointing girls to the desk to "nanny" stories, as if even as editors women were no more than baby-sitters and editorial maids.

Frank's reaction to his increasing awareness of discrimination was to make fun of himself as the clueless white male.

In the corporate world we covered, blacks and women were often almost invisible. When Warren and Martha would come across pictures of all-white-male boards of directors or all-white-male galleries of the nation's highest paid executives, they would rip them out and tape them to posts in the Business newsroom with "What's wrong with this picture?" scrawled across them.

"Looks good to me," Frank would say. "Where's the lead on that story?"

Initially, we were all just good colleagues together on the financial staff. There were no special ties among us. But they began developing as we worked together.

[3]

The Three of Us

The financial staff had been forced to relocate for two years to a corner of Style. But in 1995 we were moving back to our refurbished space in the main newsroom, and there was no question that the three of us would be sitting together. Frank picked out the best real estate, a sunny corner by the window overlooking the Russian Embassy. The three of us moved in to a three-desk cluster that Frank named "the Elder Pod" in reference to our seniority on the staff.

How did we come to be so close? It's a long story—or rather, several stories. Some of them we wrote together. Some of them we lived together. Some were terrifying and sad. But the laughter and the friendship that we shared kept us going through career highs, personal lows, and brushes with death.

The *Washington Post* is a place of quietly enforced boundaries, scripted social distances. The atmosphere can be convivial, as it often is early mornings before the newsroom goes into full roar. But, mostly, it's competitive.

Assignment editors compete for the attentions and blessings of their bosses, the assistant managing editors. The assistant managing editors vie for nods from their superiors, the executive editors, and reporters fight with one another for the attention of any editor they can get.

Trust is a curious commodity in such an environment. Editors must have faith in their reporters, and reporters must believe that their editors are backing them to get stories into the newspaper. The publisher must trust that the editors and reporters know what they're doing.

But that trust can break down, on a personal level, under the pressures of competition. Trusting a colleague with a story idea or with a tidbit of information to help advance a story can be hard. How do you know that the colleague won't try to take credit?

Overcoming competitiveness is uncommon in a culture where individual bylines determine careers.

Rarer still is the kind of trust that turns partners into

friends who celebrate one another's victories and who are there for one another, as a matter of course, in moments of sadness and pain.

The three of us developed that kind of friendship. We were the Elder Pod, three aging, ink-stained Musketeers, all for one and one for all in a workplace where being for one's self was the natural order of the day.

The bond wasn't instant, though we all liked each other from the start. We were grateful to Frank for bringing us to the Business section and admired him as an editor. Then, as we worked together, we grew closer to Frank and to each other.

It's hard to pick apart the threads in a cloth of friendship that's become so tightly woven. But some of the elements included shared values, shared bylines, and—increasingly—shared trust.

One issue that brought us closer together was labor relations. Frank had covered labor. Warren had covered labor. And Martha and Warren were both active in the Newspaper Guild, our union at the *Post*.

In 1983, Martha was cochair of the union bargaining committee. Labor relations at the *Post* had been poisoned by the 1975 press operators' strike and were still strained. There had been an attempt to oust the union. It had survived, but it was badly weakened. Every subsequent round of contract negotiations was a long struggle, creating more bitterness among *Post* employees whose raises were deferred.

The most recent contract had expired in July 1982, and negotiations were dragging on again. When Martha came back to her desk after bargaining sessions, Frank was always curious to hear what had happened at the bargaining table. Frank is a born negotiator, a skilled negotiator, a compulsive negotiator. He loved bargaining, whether it was trading employees with another newsroom staff, buying a car, or negotiating a contract. In an earlier job as a reporter with a wire service, he had bargained on the union side.

Often Frank would suggest new approaches for deadlocked issues, and many of his ideas were helpful. There was some grumbling among other committee members over the frequent talks between Frank, who was management, and Martha. But anyone who knew Frank knew that he was trying to resolve the dispute, not carrying water for management.

Frank and other managers were worried about the state of labor relations. At the Pugwash meeting that year (an annual gathering of the newspaper's top executives), National Editor Leonard Downie, Jr., and Foreign Editor Jim Hoagland had talked about how labor relations were corroding the atmosphere at the *Post*. They urged Frank to raise the issue with Bradlee, which he did. "Why don't you talk to Don Graham?" was Bradlee's suggestion. Donald E. Graham, now chairman of the Washington Post Corporation, was the publisher of the *Post*.

As the process wore on, Frank and national security reporter Mike Getler encouraged management to reach an agreement with the Guild. Finally, an agreement was reached, and it was approved by the union in November 1983. In the meantime, Frank and Martha had developed a closer friendship.

Something else was going on about that time. Frank began taking hours away from the newsroom for doctors' visits. Frank had a hard time talking about anything personal, and he didn't say anything to anyone in the financial section about what was happening during this period. But he had been diagnosed with leukemia, and his life was in danger.

Frank was embarrassed by his illness. He didn't want to be viewed as weak, as a liability, or as an object of pity. He didn't even tell his sisters initially, planning only to send them a letter the night before surgery, until his wife Otey insisted he call them.

Martha was clueless, consumed by her own career and its daily challenges. As local business editor, she had been having problems with a copy editor, so one day she did what she often did. She took her problems to Frank, stepping into his office, shutting the door, and launching into her complaints.

"I have leukemia," Frank said.

Martha's eyes immediately filled with tears.

"If this is your idea of how to cheer people up," she said, "you're not doing a very good job." Frank threw a box of tissues at her.

Martha sat with her back to the glass, wiping her eyes, listening to the details. She stayed until she could walk out of his office without sobbing. He swore her to secrecy. She was the first of his colleagues in whom he confided the bad news.

Frank had been diagnosed with leukemia on March 8, 1984, at 1:30 P.M. It was a turning point in his life, an event that made him emotionally more available to people. "It alters how you view your relationship with others," he said. He had his spleen removed in 1986 and went through a lengthy recuperation. He also made some choices. One was that he didn't want to spend the time he had left worrying about logistical and administrative matters, so he went back to reporting.

By then, Martha had returned to reporting, too. Martha was covering the airline beat. Frank was covering labor for the National staff. It was a period of mergers and consolidations and terrible labor unrest in the airline industry. Eastern Air Lines went on strike, and the workers were locked in mortal combat with the much-reviled airline owner Frank Lorenzo. Frank and Martha were working late nights and long weeks and loving it.

They spent much of the next six years covering airline stories together in a flawless partnership. If Martha was at the keyboard writing and left to take a call, Frank would take up where she left off. It didn't matter who was writing. Each was completely comfortable with what the other did. When Martha got advance word that Eastern would be shutting down forever on January 19, 1991, she wrote the lead of a joint story: "Eastern flew into oblivion last night," and then hopped on a plane, leaving the rest of the writing to Frank.

She flew to Atlanta, one of Eastern's major operation centers, and caught a flight from there to Miami, where it had its headquarters. On the Miami flight, the captain told passengers about the shutdown, talked about his long career with Eastern, and declared the drinks "on the house." Then the aircraft began its descent to the airport and touched down on the runway. No sooner had it touched down than it took off again. A few passengers gasped.

The pilot wanted to take one last swing around the air-port for old time's sake, he said over the intercom. The flight landed safely after a second descent, and Martha called Frank with the anecdote to use as the "kicker"—the end of the story.

A few years later, Warren and Frank embarked on another reporting partnership covering the automotive industry. It evolved into the same kind of seamless relationship shared by Frank and Martha.

Frank was addicted to scoops, and Warren had a good one in early spring 1992. A top executive of General Motors Corporation had told him that Robert C. Stempel, the company's chairman, was about to lose his job. Stempel's lieutenants, longtime GM stalwarts, were on the skids, too.

GM's board wanted a change, the executive told Warren after a company board meeting in New York. The company was losing billions of dollars annually. Its labor-management relations were the worst in the domestic auto industry. Its cars and trucks were stale.

The once complacent directors of GM were upset, and they let Stempel know it at the New York meeting.

"Bob's been given an ultimatum," the GM executive told Warren. "He's either got to fix things, or leave, and he doesn't have a lot of time."

Frank lit up at the news. He'd been a reporter at heart even when he was an editor; and now that he was a full-time reporter again, he was hungry for stories. Stories on anybody's beat would do, as long as they were good stories. He had been a journalist for decades and had covered so many areas that he was expert enough to stomp around in any reporter's territory.

Rare was the reporter who resented his intervention. He always brought more to the story than would have been there had he not gotten involved. His excitement over the GM scoop excited Warren and made him want to dig deeper, faster.

They worked together on the GM story for nearly a year, often beating the *Wall Street Journal* and usually trouncing the *New York Times*. Those were heady days for both of them.

Their GM work was nominated for a Pulitzer Prize, which they thought they had a good shot at winning. They didn't. The prize went to the *Wall Street Journal,* which often had trailed the *Post*'s coverage.

Warren was bitter about that. It was a bitterness made nastier by the racial baggage he had carried around all of his life but, until then, thought that he had packed away.

He had been second-guessed by white people since childhood. He had met white Catholics who marveled over his pronunciation and understanding of liturgical Latin. He had cleaned the houses of white owners who expressed shock that he actually read books. In the early days of the

---

GM coverage, when he and Frank were beating everyone on the story, he frequently was ridiculed by white journalists who accused him of being "used" and "spoon-fed" by black company sources who had a grudge against GM. Ironically, the same journalists praised the industriousness of white peers who engineered scoops on the story.

"Damned Pulitzer committee just couldn't believe that a black guy could do that kind of business reporting," Warren thought, and said as much to Frank.

Frank was disappointed, too. But he wasn't angry. He responded to Warren's racial charge with two sentences.

"I'm white. They didn't give the prize to me, either," he said, and left it at that.

Later, Frank said it really didn't matter why they didn't win the Pulitzer. "It's not the end of your life; nor is it the end of mine," he said to Warren. "Life is more important than that."

[4]

Life Is More Important Than That

Frank was right. By the time Warren discovered in 1995 that he had severe hypertension and possible life-threatening damage to his kidneys, we had all been through personal crises that taught us how important relationships are.

While Frank had been battling leukemia, both Warren and Martha were wrestling with wrenching family problems.

Warren, who was writing a column about cars in addition to his reporting duties, was often called away to deal with his son's difficulties. His oldest son, Tony, was having academic and disciplinary problems at Yorktown Senior

High School. Tony had previously been diagnosed with a seizure disorder, which he passionately denied he had. As a result, he stopped taking his medicine, throwing it under the bed. Warren and Mary Anne found out when he suffered a seizure; tests at the hospital showed only a trace of the medication in his system.

Tony's rage against his disabilities was made deeper by the contrast with his high-achieving sisters, Binta and Kafi. Tony brought home failing or barely passing grades. The girls brought home A's and B's and honor-roll citations. Binta and Kafi were preparing for an Ivy League college. Tony was struggling just to get out of high school and into an uncertain future.

The sibling battles generated by those differences turned into full-scale war in 1991, after Binta had enrolled at Barnard College in New York, leaving Kafi at home to bear the brunt of Tony's wrath. This bothered Warren. Tony could be violent. But Kafi was no pacifist, either. He feared that the two eventually might get into a fight that might leave one or both of them seriously injured, or dead.

Warren's fears were heightened one Friday afternoon when he returned home to find Kafi sulking on a sofa in the living room, while Tony was out back banging a hammer on the patio and muttering, "I'm going to get her back. I'm going to get her back."

The situation was saved by a red Pontiac Firebird, a test car Warren had driven home. He invited Tony to "go for a ride." Tony quickly dropped the hammer, completely forgetting his rage for the moment. The ride ended at an Arlington County mental health facility not far from the house. Warren reported Tony's behavior to officials and described his son's increasingly violent behavior. He asked that Tony be committed. It was a very hard thing for a father to do. But it was easier than attending a funeral for Tony or Kafi.

Warren's worries about Tony frequently distracted him during the workday. There were protracted telephone conversations with doctors and others about what was going on. Sitting at the next desk, Martha couldn't help but hear, and after the phone conversations, Warren would often turn to Martha and describe what was happening. And since Warren and Frank were working on some of the same stories, Frank had to know when Warren would need to be away.

With the strain of dealing with the situation at home, Warren often was distracted and would forget to tell his editor that he would be away or late. When Frank and Martha knew, they would pass on the information to the editor, who didn't know Warren well and was suspicious of his absences. Warren didn't need the extra hassle.

———

About the same time, Martha's daughter Sarah was going through the adolescence from hell. Beautiful and easily passing for eighteen at age twelve, she had begun running into problems almost immediately when she went to junior high school.

Now she was falling apart both academically and emotionally, and she began losing consciousness and falling down. "Mom. It's happening again," she said in a late afternoon phone call to the *Post*. When Martha arrived at the house, the back porch was littered with broken glass. Sarah's boyfriend had refused to leave and had threatened to commit suicide if they broke up. Sarah didn't remember much after that, nor could she say how she had cut herself.

That was only the beginning of a dangerous downward spiral. Sarah was hanging out with other troubled kids and often disappeared for a day or two, sleeping in abandoned houses.

She went through a series of terrifying diagnoses—epilepsy, brain tumor, brain disorder, schizophrenia, and borderline personality disorder. Warren had been through a similar pattern of diagnoses with Tony, which made it easier for Martha to talk to him about Sarah's problems. It's agonizing to talk even to close friends and family when you have fears for your children, much less to anyone else. But Warren had been there, done that. And Frank was Frank, a comforter who always had the right words and who often had the right advice.

By April 1992, after Sarah wound up in Georgetown University Hospital's emergency room for an overdose of antidepressants, Martha and Hamilton hospitalized her at Sheppard Pratt Hospital against her will for depression.

It was an unimaginably painful decision, compounded by the fear that it might not work. Driving home from the hospital, where they had left a furious Sarah, both Martha and Hamilton cried quietly. And it was about to get worse.

Sarah terrified the staff at Sheppard Pratt for a week or two. She wouldn't see her parents initially and told the staff that she had hit her dad, which wasn't true. After a short time there, however, Sarah suddenly became incredibly cooperative. She played softball. She went on hikes. The more the staff told Martha how well Sarah was doing, the more terrified Martha was that Sarah would con and charm the staff into thinking she was fine.

Martha's fears, sadly, were justified. Sarah had a plan. She had been checking out the grounds during those softball games and hikes, looking for ways to escape. Sarah and her parents met with a social worker for a family therapy session one morning. After the session, walking to class with the social worker, Sarah asked to be trusted to return to class by herself. She seemed so believable, the social worker said.

———

Martha was home, still trying to brace herself to go to work, when she got the call from the social worker: Sarah had "eloped."

In the following terrifying weeks, Martha didn't know whether she would ever see Sarah again. Martha's husband was often working and away from the house during the weeks that followed. It was hard for Martha to go to work, and harder still to talk about what was going on. Martha told Frank, who told management as much as they needed to know to understand when she didn't show up.

Fortunately, Sarah stayed in touch with Veronica DeNegri, the mother of one of her former boyfriends. Veronica insisted that Sarah call her parents. She did, and they brokered an uneasy truce.

Sarah and Martha both survived her adolescence, but it was touch and go. And though it was the most important problem Martha was dealing with, it wasn't the only one. During the same time period, her brother-in-law, Rick, was dying, and Martha was trying to provide some support for him, her sister JE, and her nephew Russell. Russell was only eight when his dad died in October 1993. Richard Manning Ricks had struggled through surgery for brain tumors and kidney failure with his family's support, but in the end the disease overwhelmed them.

At the same time, Martha's marriage was falling apart.

She planned to leave in 1993, then changed her mind when Hamilton asked her to stay. "I want you to say you're not going to leave," he had said. Then he left in 1994, and they divorced in 1995.

In 1995, still dealing with the divorce, Martha also had to help her brother Malcolm and her mother. She had visited Houston and noticed how frail Malcolm was and had persuaded her mother to get him to a doctor for tests.

Malcolm, who was forty-six, had told his doctor that Martha and his mother should make the decisions about his care, so it was Martha whom the doctor called with the diagnosis: advanced AIDS and AIDS-related dementia. With difficulty, Martha picked up the phone to tell her mother and then flew back to Houston. Two weeks later, the doctor called again, asking her to agree to withhold all care except for keeping him comfortable and clean. After a consultation with her mother, she did. In the meantime, Frank was helping her make arrangements to fly to Houston again.

During all the pain and sorrow, Frank and Warren provided critical support. Sarah helped, too. It had taken several years, but the closeness Martha and Sarah had shared for most of Sarah's life gradually had been restored. Sarah was loving and supportive of both her parents throughout the separation and divorce.

Hamilton wanted to separate but didn't want to tell Sarah. Martha told her anyway. Sarah had responded that day with hugs and kisses, cups of hot tea, and encouraging advice. "You can have adventures, Mom," she said. "You can hop freight trains. You can have a great time."

JE was a blessing during the difficult years, too. And so were many long-time friends from outside of the office— Alice and Phil Shabecoff, Carol Stoel, Colby King, Darla Hamilton, Eric Lueders and Thad Logan, Johnnie Lu Zarecor, Kathy Seddon, Mary Ponder, Neil Bernstein, Richard and Susana O'Mara, and Tracy and Dick Guy. But Frank and Warren were the day-in, day-out buffers, the ones who would distract Martha with a joke if a telephone conversation left her crying, the ones who kept her welfare constantly in mind, consulting with each other behind her back about what they needed to do.

At the rock-bottom of her depression, they were even calling her at home.

One morning, unable to get out of bed even to walk the dogs, Martha reached for the ringing phone. It was Warren. "Frank made me call," he said sheepishly. That was all it took to get her moving again—the knowledge that they cared that much.

To understand the power of that phone call, you have to understand that we didn't socialize outside of the newsroom, and we didn't call each other at home unless it was work-related. The phone call was a step outside the bounds of our friendship-as-normal.

For weeks afterward, if Martha forgot to mention that she had a morning assignment, and walked into the office later in the morning than usual, Warren would look up, embarrassed. "Uh, you might have a message on your phone at home. We were just wondering where you were."

"I was out on assignment," Martha would say. "You can call off the suicide watch."

[5]

Hypertension

Warren's Story

Mommie died February 13, 1995, at 7:15 P.M. She died in a hospital hallway moments after walking out of Daddy's room at Touro Infirmary in New Orleans, where he was being treated for Black Man's Diseases. That's what blacks call them, anyway. It's a rubric that includes hypertension, diabetes, diverticulosis, cirrhosis of the liver, and the general strain of being black in America.

Clinically, the condition involves the organic and mental effects of chronic racism—the endless tension, often subtle, stemming from worry over whether you will be accepted, rejected, belittled, or ignored because of the color of your skin.

Daddy and Mommie struggled with racism in different ways. Daddy was a perfectionist. He never allowed himself the luxury of failure. It was as if any mistake on his part reflected on all black people, their intelligence and morality.

Mommie was sneaky. She loved the white nuns and some of the white priests. In fact, she ignored their whiteness altogether. She loved Jews, whom she considered fellow victims of ethnic hatred, and whom she did not regard as being white. But Mommie never was comfortable around White Anglo-Saxon Protestants. With them, she put on a show, feigning niceness in their presence but damning them to hell behind their backs.

Both Mommie and Daddy had hypertension, more commonly known as high blood pressure. Both had diabetes. Both had pulmonary disorders. Daddy suffered a stroke in his late seventies that left him practically blind in his right eye. Mommie died from a massive heart attack outside of Daddy's hospital room. She was seventy-one.

Mommie worshiped Daddy. I believe she really died because she couldn't live without him. She tried to save him by herself, taking care of his medical needs, driving him back and forth to the doctor and the hospital, and covering up the severity of his condition in upbeat telephone reports to her surviving children, all of whom had taken jobs outside of Louisiana.

"I did not want to worry you all," she told me, when I visited New Orleans shortly before her death. Daddy was asleep in one of the back bedrooms of my parents' brick, typically suburban, ranch-style home. He was sleeping a lot in those days. The place felt lonely. Mommie was alone. Life's tables were turned. She had always depended on Daddy. Now, he was entirely dependent on her. "I think I'm going to lose him," she said.

But she would have none of that. She went first. She died in the arms of my youngest sister, Mary Edith, who had gone to New Orleans to help Mommie with Daddy.

"Mommie was smiling when she died," Mary Edith said the day after the fatal heart attack. "She was dressed to the nines, had on a pretty dress and everything, and she was smiling."

It figures. Mommie always put great store in personal appearance. There was no way she was going to make a last visit to Daddy and take a trip to Heaven looking shabby.

I wasn't feeling so good, though. I had spent the week before Mommie's death traveling. I was barely home for two hours in Arlington, Virginia, when all three of my sisters called to tell Mary Anne and me about Mommie's death. I had a splitting headache when I arrived in New Orleans the next day.

My sister-in-law, Jayne (with the "y," please) Henderson

Dickens-Brown, had arrived earlier. Jayne is a Philadelphia physician who comes from a family of doctors. "You don't look too well," she told me after I settled into a guest room.

"Death will do that to you," I said. But Jayne is used to dealing with smart-asses. She married my brother Bobby, after all.

"Maybe I ought to check your blood pressure," Jayne said.

"Maybe you should just give me an aspirin. I have a headache," I said.

Jayne has an intimidating way of raising her right eyebrow when she thinks you're being really stupid. She raised her right eyebrow.

"I'm going to check your pressure," she said. "You Browns are crazy people. All of you have high blood pressure. None of you will do anything about it. That's why all of you die from strokes and heart attacks."

She had made her point. I stretched out my right arm. Jayne wrapped a pressure cuff a tad above my right elbow and began squeezing the rubber bulb, all the while looking intently at the blood pressure monitoring gauge. I felt as if I was taking a test. I guess I was, and I flunked it.

"160 over 95!" Jayne yelled. "You've got to see your doctor."

"You are a doctor," I said. "Write a prescription or something." Oops! That made her angry.

"I can't just write you a prescription. I'm a doctor in Pennsylvania, not Louisiana. I'm not your personal doctor. You need to make an appointment with your personal care physician and get a full examination, you butt!"

I had absolutely no intention of following her advice, partly because Jayne was such a debutante that it was difficult for me to take her seriously as a doctor, but also because Jayne was right: No one in my family of hypertensives ever took high blood pressure seriously.

We had a fatalist, self-defeating way of dealing with the disease. So did most of our black friends in Louisiana. We'd eat highly seasoned gumbo, and take blood-pressure pills. We'd drink multiple bottles of Jax, Falstaff, Dixie, or Regal beer and take pressure pills.

Boudin, crab cakes, crayfish, étouffée, jambalaya, shrimp —hey, cher, it didn't matter. We'd wash it all down with beer, liquor, or heavily sugared lemonade. If "the pressure" got high, we just popped some pressure pills. Laissez les bon temps roulez! Let the good times roll, baby!

High blood pressure was like the Mississippi River. It just kept on keeping on. You didn't worry about it. It was just one of those things, like racism or breathing.

Mommie often nagged Daddy about his pressure. Her fussing was confusing. She'd nag, and then fix him a bowl of gumbo. She'd nag, and then prepare a Sunday feast of fried chicken, highly seasoned potato salad, and spicy mustard greens. We all joined Daddy in consuming the contradiction.

My siblings and I went to Touro to visit Daddy hours after Mommie's funeral. He was too ill to attend services. We assured him that all went well. But he had other concerns. "How much did it cost?" he asked me.

Whenever Daddy had questions about money, he always asked me or DaLinda, the oldest of the girls. He called us his "little black Jews." Daddy wasn't anti-Semitic. He was quite the opposite. To him, Jews were the people who had it all together. They had overcome centuries of brutal oppression to build a place for themselves in the world. Jews took care of their own people and they took care of their money, and they valued education. Daddy often urged us to emulate the Jews. Whenever he called me a Jew, he meant it as a compliment.

Mommie's last rites cost $10,500. Daddy was happy with that news. "Never let them take advantage of dying to put you in debt," he said. "It's stupid to put money in the ground." Daddy's "them," like Mommie's, were non-Jewish, mostly non-Catholic white people—and unscrupulous blacks who did their bidding.

A young, black nurse passed me as I was leaving Daddy's room. I asked her to take my blood pressure. She complied.

"Borderline," she said after doing the pressure check. I deliberately didn't ask what "borderline" meant. I only knew that it sounded better than what Jayne was saying. I chose to go with the "good" news.

But the news turned bad again nine months later. I was sitting in the office of Dr. Devra C. Marcus in Washington, D.C. She was not happy. I had been sent to her minutes earlier by a woman dentist who refused to treat me because my blood pressure was too high, 170/120. The dentist worked in the same building as Dr. Marcus. Neither woman would let me leave the place until my pressure dropped.

"That is more than borderline or slightly abnormal," Dr. Marcus said, confirming the dentist's pressure reading. "That is dangerous. You could have a stroke. You probably already have organ damage."

I looked at her incredulously. Another alarmist, I thought. But Dr. Marcus was insistent. "I want you to hear me," she said. "This can kill you. It will kill you, if it goes untreated. You can die from a heart attack or a stroke. You can die from kidney failure. Hypertension destroys organs. It's why we call it the 'silent killer.'"

She sounded like Jayne, which made me more angry than scared. "Damn it, lady," I thought. "I just wanted to get my teeth fixed. Give me some pressure pills and shut up."

Dr. Marcus gave me some emergency doses of a blood-pressure drug. Something called Procardia, I think. She made me rest on a cot in a room adjacent to her office. But I was up thirty minutes later, ready to return to work at the *Post*. Dr. Marcus had other ideas.

"You're going home," she said. "I've already called [then–financial editor David] Ignatius. I told him that you cannot possibly return to work today." She had treated David Ignatius and a number of other people at the *Post*, which she called "a stressful working environment."

I protested. Dr. Marcus refused to back off.

"This is very, very serious," Dr. Marcus said. "I want you back here next week."

"Yeah, right lady," I thought. "I'll call you."

I went back to work anyway; but Ignatius suggested that I "take it easy" and go home. Dr. Marcus had prevailed.

A week later, I felt fine. I had no headaches. A new blood-pressure medication, a drug called Verapamil, was working. But that was a guess. During that first meeting in her office, Dr. Marcus had asked me to keep a twice-daily check of my blood pressure, using one of those readily available blood-pressure monitors found in drugstores. I never bought the monitor, never did the checks. Dr. Marcus was not amused.

She began the follow-up visit with a stern lecture.

"You're not helping me do my job!" she said, nearly shouting. "You're not being fair, Warren." I hate it when a woman says something like that. It makes me feel guilty and all messed-up inside. I really hate it if the woman is short and cute. Such women always seem especially hurt when they accuse you of being "unfair." Mary Anne is short and cute. Dr. Marcus is short and cute. Dr. Marcus was using the "Mary Anne effect," and it worked.

"You're being stupid," Dr. Marcus scolded. "Very stupid, and very unfair. You want to do a good job at the *Post*. Well, this is my job, and I want to do a good job, too. But you're working against me. I can't help you if you won't work with me," she said.

That really was the "Mary Anne effect." It sounded like a marriage proposal, or a mandate to renew my commitment to marriage. "Damn, lady," I thought. "I don't want a commitment. I just want you to fix what's broken and get it over with."

Dr. Marcus wanted a commitment.

"Look, this is the deal," she said. "You probably already have kidney damage. You could even have heart damage. The damage may be irreversible. That means you can have a fatal heart attack or lose your kidneys. That means might have to go on dialysis or get a transplant."

She got my attention. Dr. Marcus outlined my immediate medical future: Frequent urine and blood tests to check creatinine levels to determine how well my kidneys were functioning. High levels meant kidney malfunction. Low levels meant that the kidneys were okay.

I did the first group of tests. The results came back a few days later. I wasn't okay. My creatinine levels were high. My blood pressure was up again, too—158/102. Things didn't look good at all.

Dr. Marcus said my renal function was severely compromised. She ordered me off red meats and other high-protein foods. Damaged kidneys have difficulty processing protein.

That day, November 28, 1995, is fixed in my mind. I was shaken by Dr. Marcus's medical report. I needed an office fix. The office is a buffer zone between me and home, which is why I returned to the office before going home to Mary Anne. So, I went to the office and logged onto my e-mail, which is always stuffed with letters from readers asking about cars and trucks. Answering those e-mails gave me a sense of power. I was doing something, solving other people's problems while simultaneously ignoring my own. Doing the mail gave me time I needed to work the shock out of my system, to prepare a mask. I knew that Mary Anne would pepper me with questions as soon as I walked through the front door of our house. She did, without hesitation.

"Hi, honey. What did the doctor say?" Mary Anne asked as soon as I opened the door. I didn't even have time to put down my satchel.

"She told me to change my diet," I responded. Nice strategy, I thought. Mary Anne always is after me to change my diet. Give her an early victory in this interrogation, and she won't feel the need to pursue the matter further, not tonight anyway. I was right. But instead, I got an hour-long lecture on my New Orleans eating habits. It was painful, but worth the trade for what the conversation might have been.

I started trying to do the right thing. I ate the right foods at home, and cheated like hell at work. I ate business dinners of plausible deniability. It worked like this. I might order a steak, but I also ordered lots of vegetables. That way, I was ready for Mary Anne when I returned home. "What did you eat?" she asked. "Lots of vegetables," I said. That way, I wasn't telling a lie. I just wasn't telling her the whole truth. What the hell, lawyers, politicians, journalists, priests, and doctors do it all the time.

"Am I going to die?" a terminally ill patient asks a doctor. "That's hard to say," the doctor says. "There are other things we can do."

Bullshit. How can it be "hard to say" that someone is going to die? Everybody dies. At least my culinary half-truths to Mary Anne had substance. What did I eat? Lots of vegetables. It wasn't my fault that she didn't ask about the meat.

But it's hard to fool Mary Anne. She knew something was up. She fed me oatmeal in the mornings before I went to work. She gave me meatless, salt-less, sugarless dinners on those nights when I didn't eat out. She began monitoring the number of nights I did eat out, and she fed me next to nothing sinful on weekends when she could watch me closely. It was the culinary equivalent of hell. But I wound up losing weight in spite of myself.

My blood pressure also fell in the first three months of 1996. Nearly normal pressure readings of 133/81, or something similar, were frequent. But part of that was attributable to yet another blood-pressure drug, Vasotec. It dropped my pressure, all right. But the drug was a disaster in other ways. It gave me a persistent cough.

By the spring of 1996, things were looking good. Dr. Marcus said my hypertension was "nearly adequately controlled." I guess she wanted to protect me from irrational exuberance.

She had good reason to be cautious: those damned blood and urine tests. Dr. Marcus didn't like what she was seeing. My creatinine levels were soaring. She estimated that my kidneys were "about 30 percent efficient" in removing toxins from my bloodstream. I was slowly poisoning myself.

In early December 1997, I did several twenty-four-hour urine tests, which involved bringing big, amber urine bottles home on weekends and peeing into them every time I had to take a whiz.

The news wasn't good from those tests, as indicated by Dr. Marcus's notes on one of them: "Mr. Brown's 24-hour urine test was abnormal," she wrote. She also noted that my blood pressure and weight were up again.

A new year rolled around. I vowed to make a change. I would drop 40 pounds and get down to the target weight of 145–150 pounds for my 5' 7" body. I would eat what Mary Anne served, and I would not cheat in the food lines at the office cafeteria or during expense-account meals. I would become a new man.

But by the next New Year, 1999, I was close to becoming a dead man.

Under an arrangement with Dr. Marcus and a Dr. Mark Guzman at Georgetown University Hospital, I agreed to do certain medical checks before leaving town on news assignments. This was a precautionary deal put into effect because my kidneys continued to fail.

During one of those checkups, Dr. Guzman went ballistic. He said my potassium levels were high enough to cause a fatal heart attack. I thought about Mommie. I'd hate to die and go to Heaven to be greeted by her frowning face.

"Boy, you're not supposed to be here now," she'd say. "Daddy and I need some time alone. We weren't expecting you this early."

Daddy had died June 20, 1996. On the morning of his death, he asked his caretaker to give him a haircut, a shave, and a bath. He then asked my middle sister, Loretta Marie, to help him get into his new pajamas. He also asked for his new slippers, and he requested that his caretaker slick back his hair, the way he wore it as a young man. When all was done, according to Loretta, who witnessed the scene, "Daddy turned toward Mommie's picture on the wall and stopped breathing."

My oldest brother, Danny, had died before Mommie and Daddy at age thirty-nine, about twelve years after coming home from Vietnam, where he had completed two tours of duty. At times he had slept in fields of Agent Orange, a highly toxic defoliant used to clear jungles to make it easier to see and kill the people who wanted to see and kill him.

Danny developed colon cancer, but his doctors said he died from a heart attack. My parents were devastated by his death. But they never talked much about it afterward. So Danny already was up there with them. "Sorry, Mommie," I thought while being held captive in the hospital under Dr. Guzman's watch, "I guess there's no getting away from your children."

———

The hospital admitted me for surgery. Dr. Guzman recommended that a catheter be implanted in my chest for emergency dialysis. For long-term dialysis, he asked the surgeons to install a fistula, a joining together of two smaller veins to create a super-vein to speed the flow of blood in my left arm, where dialysis needles would be inserted. The increased pressure forces the blood through the needles, into the dialysis tubes, and through the machine's mechanical kidney. The doctors gave me a laxative to flush out the excessive potassium.

There was another thing: I would need a kidney transplant. Mary Anne told me that when I awakened from surgery.

"They said you're going to need another kidney. I'm giving you one of mine," she said.

Typical Mary Anne, I thought. She never sidestepped or backtracked when it came to helping me or our children. She just did whatever she thought needed doing.

But her instant decision to give me a kidney worried me. Just because she was my wife didn't mean she would be a suitable donor. Mary Anne doesn't handle rejection well. She'd go nuts if her kidney didn't work out. I knew she'd be deeply wounded if that happened, and I didn't want that.

Mary Anne was a match. Her type O-negative blood

made her a universal blood donor. We also shared two compatible antigens, substances that produce antibodies, out of a possible perfect match of six. That was a pretty good outcome for a couple of randomly selected mates. Many married couples have no antigen matches at all.

By June 1999, we got the go-ahead for the transplant surgery. Mary Anne was ecstatic, which I found odd. I had never seen someone so happy to bleed for someone else, and to give up a part of her body in the process. A devout Catholic, she was even saying prayers of thanksgiving. "Thank you, God, for giving me a chance to save my husband."

I had mixed feelings about Mary Anne's enthusiasm. I was happy that her gift would free me from the rigors of dialysis, which consumed twelve hours of my life every week, and which involved no small degree of pain when the dialysis technicians stopped using the chest catheter in favor of inserting two long needles into my left arm. But I was worried that she would be injured by giving up a kidney, that she would suffer some unforeseen harm, maybe die. The latter possibility scared me silly. I joined her prayers of thanksgiving, but privately I believed we were thanking God for a mixed blessing. I envied Mary Anne for her unquestioning faith.

Martha's Story

It was hard watching Warren get sick. It was harder watching him make it worse.

Warren has a way of dealing with people he doesn't like. He pretends they don't exist. And he brought that same approach to the disease that was killing him.

Frank and I were close enough to hear the excuses he made to cancel doctors' appointments and the apologies for the ones he missed. He had the time wrong in his appointment book. He had an interview. He was out of town. He thought it was next week. He would employ his excuses while turning on his telephone charm with the medical-office schedulers. "How are you, m'love? How are you this lovely day? Oh, golly gee whiz, was that today? I am so sorry."

And we could hear the other end of the dressing-downs he got from Dr. Ruth (our pod's nickname for Dr. Devra Marcus), who wasn't buying a bit of it.

Warren's first instinct when he found out that he was dying of kidney failure was to ignore it, to treat it lightly, to hope—if he just kept acting as if nothing was wrong—that it would go away. As Frank said, "He was losing control, and you could see it. And it bugged the hell out of him. Control is a big issue with Warren, and he couldn't maintain it."

Warren was way overweight and eating badly, even with hypertension, diabetes, and kidney failure. Frank and I would catch him with junk food. "This is okay. This is fine," Warren would try to argue. Then we'd make him do a dramatic reading of the ingredients listed on the back. How much salt? How many of the calories from fat? At 5'7", he weighed about 195 pounds, the same weight as Frank, who was 6 feet tall.

When he got caught, Warren would throw the half-eaten junk food into the trash basket by his desk. Into the trash they went, with only a few bites gone: moon pies, chips, ice cream bars. Warren was the vending machine's best friend.

"I've lost six pounds," he would say, stretching the oversized sweaters he favored away from his belly to show us how he'd shrunk. It was always six pounds. "That's the same six pounds you lost last week," we'd say. Frank and National Desk Copy Chief Vince Rinehart tried to enlist Warren in the walks they were taking for their health, and Warren would stop frequently, citing a need to tie his shoes. "I dance for exercise," Warren would tell us when we fussed at him.

Most of his dancing was dancing around the fact that he was in danger.

But it was easier for me to talk to Frank about how frightening Warren's behavior was than to talk to Warren.

We might both chide him, but never in a way that said to Warren how scary it was to watch what was happening. He didn't seem to take his health problems seriously enough and ignored what he needed to do to keep himself alive.

Meanwhile, he and Mary Anne searched the Internet, looking for solutions for the disease that so frightened them both.

That's how Warren almost killed himself. On the basis of something he read on the Internet, Warren diagnosed that potassium was what he needed. He started swigging a quart of orange juice a day and eating bananas. And the worse he felt, the more potassium he consumed.

We weren't expecting Warren in the office on January 15, 1999. Frank and I knew he had medical tests. But as the day wore on, with still no Warren, we were getting worried.

We had reason to be.

When he finally called, he had been checked into the ICU. The doctors at Georgetown had been so alarmed by his health that they wouldn't even let him go home for his clothes. Frank and I and our boss, Jill Dutt, climbed into Frank's car and headed for Georgetown. Warren was in the heart unit, not the kidney unit. He had raised his potassium levels so high that he had almost given himself a heart attack.

When Warren told us, we probably should have shaken

him. But we were laughing too hard as Warren described self-medicating himself from the Internet rather than talking to any of the doctors he saw on a regular basis, swilling prodigious amounts of orange juice, and eating more bananas till he damned near killed himself. "Good work, Warren. Keep it up, and you won't need to worry about that kidney at all." In retrospect, it doesn't seem that funny, but we were following the unspoken code of the Elder Pod. When life gets scary, make a joke out of it.

By the time we got back to the newsroom, everybody in the section was making jokes about Warren's ill-conceived medical career. When he came back to work, we taped a photo of a huge bunch of bananas on his computer screen.

When it became clear that Warren needed a kidney transplant, I volunteered to be tested. But I breathed a sigh of relief when Mary Anne insisted on donating one of her own kidneys to her husband. I had thought about donating a kidney before, when my brother-in-law's kidney was failing. Sadly, so many other parts of his body were under attack, from the von Hippel-Lindau disease that killed him, a kidney was beside the point.

When Warren went on dialysis the first time, he had a tough time of it. Most of his difficulties were with its restraints rather than the actual dialysis. He was frustrated by the limitations it imposed on him, especially on his ability to travel. Warren wanted to keep up his work schedule as if nothing was wrong. Nothing was wrong, was it?

The whole Business section prepared for Warren's transplant. Caroline Mayer, who sat across a divider from us and who lived near Warren and Frank in Arlington, helped organize meals to be delivered to the house after the surgery, when both Warren and Mary Anne would be recovering.

We kept an array of toys in the Elder Pod, and one of them was an inflated palm tree approximately five and a half feet tall. Volkswagen had supplied the original palm tree. It had been part of a press package, a lame gimmick to announce some automotive development. We brought in a small pump, blew it up, and it became part of our world. At Christmas, we would tape a small string of lights around it and invite the section over for a tree-lighting ceremony.

Frank and I determined that Warren needed a palm tree at home during his convalescence, so Frank contacted Volkswagen and acquired a second palm tree.

We also collected money for books and CDs for entertainment during the recuperation and bought Warren a CD player so he could have music in the hospital.

Frank was posted at the hospital during the surgery, reporting back on its progress. I was at the office, waiting for Frank's calls, which came in periodically throughout the day. Then word came back: The surgery was over, and Mary Anne's kidney was functioning in Warren's body.

It was a success, a happy ending. The recovery was long, but we breathed a sigh of relief. Warren was going to be fine.

The day he returned to work after six weeks of recuperation, we were ready for him. The *Post* hung a big sign up in front of the elevators on the fifth floor welcoming him back. And, because Warren loves to pop bubble wrap, we had laid out a carpet for him—not a red carpet but a roll of bubble wrap stretched the length of the newsroom to our desks.

That was September 1999. We believed the worst of Warren's troubles were behind us.

*Martha McNeil Hamilton,
right, with her siblings in
Houston, Texas, 1950.*

*Martha's parents, Evelyn
Sims McNeil and Bruce
McNeil, came of political
age admiring the Roosevelts.*

*Warren (in white coat)and
brother Bobby pose after mass at
Holy Redeemer Catholic Church
in New Orleans.*

*Warren's parents, the late Lillian
Gadison-Provost Brown and
Daniel Thomas Brown Sr., used
education and the Catholic
Church to combat racism.*

Martha at her first newspaper job, filing and retrieving clippings in the library at the World-Telegram & Sun *in New York City.*

Hamilton in the late 1960s, after she moved to Washington, D.C.

Warren's 1965 graduation photo from St. Augustine High School in New Orleans.

Warren working in an NAACP convention newsroom in New York. Afro hairdos were a hell of a lot cheaper than haircuts.

Martha's parents, her daughter Sarah, and Martha's aunt Mattie Sims in Houston.

Martha and her sister JE McNeil. The first time Martha thought about donating a kidney was when JE's husband Richard Manning Ricks was on dialysis.

Martha's daughter Sarah at age fifteen.

Warren and Mary Anne with (l-r) Tony, Binta, and Kafi. Circa 1980 in Arlington, Virginia.

Warren and Mary Anne at home in Arlington five months after his first kidney transplant. Mary Anne was the donor.

The "Elder Pod": Warren and Martha with colleague Frank Swoboda in the Washington Post *newsroom.*

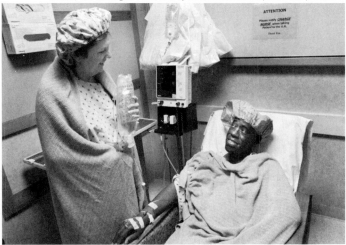

Martha and Warren posed for a final photograph just minutes before they headed toward separate operating rooms for kidney transplant surgery.

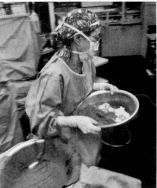

Dr. Amy Lu rushes the kidney she removed from Martha to Warren's operating room.

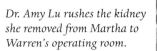

Martha visits Warren for the first time post-transplant, three days after the surgery.

[6]

Losing It

Warren's Story

Happy endings aren't forever. They're a prelude to something else. That's the way it turned out for my first kidney transplant.

But in those early months after the surgery, it seemed that happiness would last. Mary Anne and I returned to work. Home life returned to normalcy. The living room, which became an intensive care unit during our mutual recuperation, went back to being a living room. We went to the movies, which was a big treat.

For two months after the operation, I avoided large crowds to avoid the risk of infection. People carry germs.

Transplant patients on immunosuppressant drugs are particularly susceptible to those germs. A cold can become pneumonia. A scratchy throat can become a fever. An infection-related fever can damage an organ transplant.

I had to be careful—had to restrict my natural tendency to hug bodies and kiss cheeks during greetings and departures. I was a people person who became afraid of touching people. That meant staying home, which I was never good at doing for long. It was torture. I'd envy people driving along the street in front of my house. They were in their cars going somewhere. I was behind the picture window of my living room wishing I was going with them.

My isolation was broken by books, many of them bought for me by Mary Anne, who began traveling beyond the perimeter of our real estate three weeks before I could cross that border. Other books came from friends—including Martha, Frank, and Jill Dutt—and from the many bookshelves of our home.

I became a child, once again moving beyond imposed boundaries via the written word. As a boy in New Orleans, books had taken me past the "Colored Only" signs of segregation. In postsurgical recuperation, they carried me beyond unilateral quarantine.

I read Civil War history, and I lost myself in Pramoedya Ananta Toer's brilliant, four-part, fictionalized history of the making of Indonesia—*This Earth of Mankind, A Child of All Nations, Footsteps,* and *House of Glass.* I marveled over how far a person could go simply by turning a page.

Still, I wanted to hit the road. The highway has its own melody—the steady roar of traffic, the clip-clap of cars and trucks rolling over expansion joints, the rumble of eighteen-wheelers. I had always thought of vehicle traffic as an intricate ballet. I loved the precision of cars changing lanes at high speeds; the maddening but exciting movements of perfectly executed but patently illegal U-turns; the dance of intimidation between two motorists equally determined to occupy the same spot at the same time. This was high art to me. I longed to become a part of it again. But I was tethered to stark reality. For people like me, an errant germ could be as fatal as a car crash.

When my medical house arrest ended in early October 1999, I was jubilant. I traveled by car, rail, and air. Things were looking up. Mary Anne and I were optimistic. I renewed my vows to take better care of myself.

My daily medical regimen included swallowing a battalion of anti-rejection drugs along with various anti-viral, anti-hypertension, and anti-bacterial medicines. It seemed as if everything going into my mouth was entering to offset the effects of something else.

Drugs were scheduled throughout my day, beginning at

6 A.M. and ending at 10 P.M. It was a chore. But taking pills was much better than doing dialysis—a grand improvement over waking up at 5:30 every other morning to be in a dialysis chair by 7 A.M.

I had dreaded those dialysis mornings, though I publicly pretended to take them in stride. I'd get up, tape a large section of plastic wrap over the catheter in my right chest, and take a shower. Then I'd dress, pack a blanket to ward off the chill of the frequently cold dialysis lab, kiss Mary Anne, and say, "See ya later, Babes." We always said "See ya later" instead of "Goodbye"—always, even when we began dating in 1966.

Every dialysis morning, I'd pray that the day's blood-washing exercise would go well. A bad day at the dialysis lab could lead to a hospital stay, or a burial. Mary Anne knew this. I'd kiss her and say "See you later, . . ." but on those mornings, she'd respond: "Come back, okay?"

I came back at the end of every dialysis session, often feeling physically better than I had before leaving home. But there were many days during the 1999 dialysis season when I returned feeling worse, usually because I was dehydrated during the blood filtering. Dried out meant worn out. Dialysis fatigue sometimes sidelined me an entire day.

The 1999 dialysis season ended with the kidney Mary Anne gave me in July of that year. The good health that seemed to follow that miracle ended eight months later with chronic diarrhea. My relationship with what was then Georgetown's nephrology department took a dump, too.

In those days, the hospital had an unfortunate way of dealing with kidney-transplant recipients and donors. Donors were treated as parts bins. At least, that's the way Mary Anne and I saw it. In May 1999, when she was a donor candidate, everyone at Georgetown seemed to be on her side. She was seen as a special person and treated as such. We thought that would be the case after the surgery. It wasn't.

Things seemed to change just hours after that first transplant surgery, when the doctors made an initial assessment that everything had gone well. The doctors told Mary Anne that she could go home that night, if she felt up to leaving. "Yes, your wife could leave tonight. But, of course, if she doesn't feel up to it, we're not going to push her out or anything," one of the surgeons told me.

I was shocked. True, Mary Anne's kidney had been extracted through the less radical laparoscopic surgical procedure, which involved making five relatively small incisions in her abdomen. But an incision is an incision, and the woman did give up a flesh-and-blood kidney.

"Are you kidding?" I asked the surgeon who had said she could leave.

"Only if she feels up to it," the surgeon said.

"She doesn't feel up to it," I said.

"Okay," said the surgeon. "We'll see how she feels tomorrow."

Unbelievable! I felt as if we were in one of those restaurants where the time-to-departure clock starts ticking the moment you sit down to eat. In those places, waiters make multiple visits to your table, asking: "Is everything okay? Will there be anything else?"

At Georgetown, the clock started ticking on Mary Anne the moment she gave up her kidney. The hospital's version of "Is everything okay?" was "If you feel up to it, you can leave tonight!"

Mary Anne left two days later, much to the chagrin of Aetna U.S. Heatlthcare, Inc., our primary medical insurer, and Georgetown University Hospital's billing department.

The hospital allowed Mary Anne one follow-up visit before turning her over to, as one of the hospital billing people put it, "your personal care physician." To us, that was the hospital's version of a one-night stand.

I was treated a bit better. The hospital's surgery department closely followed me for three months. But after the surgeons finished with me—my wounds were healed and I was showing no signs of transplant rejection—they transferred me back to Georgetown's nephrology department.

———

The hand-off was more like a drop-off. Dr. Guzman and his assistants seemed overburdened. I felt that I was no longer a priority, that I was yesterday's news, a done deal. Getting a follow-up appointment with Guzman was difficult. I'd call his office and leave a message, but wouldn't get a call back.

In a way, the situation was perfect—and perfectly dangerous—for a reluctant patient like me. If a doctor or a member of the doctor's team didn't call me back, I took that as confirmation that everything was okay, especially if I felt okay at the moment. No news is good news, right?

No news was bad news. By February 2000, I wasn't feeling so good. I would eat and go to the toilet, eat and go to the toilet. My body was a food-processing machine working overtime, and it was wearing me out. It also was getting in the way of my work.

I'd get up at 6 A.M. and take the first group of drugs. I'd eat toast and cereal, usually oatmeal, to pad my stomach. By 7:30 A.M., I'd be on the toilet. By 9 A.M., after more drugs, my stomach would be in complete turmoil again. I would get into the office at 11 A.M., or later, or sometimes not at all. This was no way to run a business.

I finally got an audience with Dr. Guzman. He told me that my problems were the expected side effects of two of the anti-rejection drugs I was taking. He lowered one of the dosages. The stomach problems disappeared for several weeks. But soon I was running to the toilet again. I lost so much weight that Mary Anne bought me a new wardrobe.

I started calling Guzman's office again—to no avail. I took blood tests on my own and had the results sent to his office. I called again several days after the tests. I got a receptionist who said: "Mr. Brown, if there was a problem, we would've called you." Her comment, albeit dismissive, made me feel better about feeling sick. But the better feeling didn't last long. I continued running to the bathroom.

I called Dr. Guzman's office several weeks later but couldn't reach him. No wonder. He wasn't there. Nor were any of his assistants. They had left Georgetown University Hospital after it was taken over by MedStar Health, a nonprofit, community-based healthcare organization serving the Baltimore/Washington region. Guzman didn't write or call me to say he was leaving. He didn't send flowers or cards. The dude just scooted. I was jilted. Georgetown turned me over to Dr. Joyce Gonin, a compassionate but tough nephrologist who insists on seeing her patients frequently.

I met with Dr. Gonin in May 2000. Initially, the meeting was contentious. Dr. Gonin started lecturing me about missing appointments. Her work was saving lives, she said, and she would not work with patients who interfered with her mission. She reminded me of Dr. Marcus, my tenacious personal doctor.

But I was in no mood to hear Dr. Gonin's reprimands. I had long ago reformed. I had kept my appointments with Guzman, such as they were, I told her. I didn't miss anything. I was the one who constantly called Guzman's office, not vice versa. Dr. Gonin relented after my rebuttal. Her entire mood changed. She said nothing about Guzman, and nothing about my complaints about what I viewed as too few office visits. "We will do things differently," she said. "You will see me every two weeks, or whatever is required."

She kept her word, and I kept mine. But what Dr. Gonin saw during those first visits wasn't pretty. I had all kinds of problems. I was falling apart.

My first anti-rejection therapy was based largely on my self-description as an African American. Clinical studies show that blacks generally have stronger immune systems than whites and thus are more likely to reject foreign organs, such as transplanted kidneys. Doctors, as a result, tend to prescribe more aggressive anti-rejection drugs, immunosuppressants, for blacks.

That's fine, if you're black with no admixture. But rare is the "African American" from Louisiana or any of the other plantation states who can make that claim.

Mommie was black French Creole. In her case, that

meant she was a mixture of West Indian, French, Irish, and Coushatta Indian. Her genetic family stemmed from so many different ethnic groups that it was a little United Nations. Well, maybe not so united. We had white people in our family who pretended that they never heard of us, and we had black family members who passed for white and pretended that they didn't know us, either.

Daddy also came from an ethnically mixed group. His ancestors were Madagascan Muslims who were sold into slavery by Madagascans who didn't want Muslims in Madagascar. Daddy's people were slaves in Mississippi, where nature took various courses and led to mating with Natchez Trace Indians.

If there were white people in Daddy's family, they were hidden well. His sisters would talk about their biological and familial links to the Natchez Indians, and they would brag ad infinitum about their Madagascan roots. But mixing with white people, if it came about at all in their family, never was discussed.

Mary Anne's people took the prize in the interracial sweepstakes. Her grandfather was so light-skinned that whites often mistook him for one of them and confided in him information that they wouldn't have shared with blacks in his hometown of Muskogee, Oklahoma. As a result, he often knew of plans that would disadvantage the black community, such as proposals for new thoroughfares through black neighborhoods or schemes to try to stop integration. Based on family legend and rumor, Mary Anne's family is part black, part Irish, and part Seminole. There might be someone else in the woodpile, but we've long ago stopped searching.

Heck, Mary Anne alone is a multipurpose minority. At some times during the year, usually during the winter, her skin is so light that some whites mistake her for white; Spanish-speaking people speak to her in Spanish; some Asians and some Arabic-speaking people mistake her for one of their own, too.

As a child, Mary Anne's coloring was her enemy. Identifiable black kids harassed her for being "high yellow" and "light, bright, damned near white." White people castigated her as a "mixed-breed," a "quadroon," and an "octoroon." But at least, as one friend put it, "she was spared being called an Oreo [cookie], because Oreos are black on the outside and white in the middle. But Mary Anne is white on the outside and black in the middle."

As an adult, however, Mary Anne's color stood us in good stead, especially when it came to buying houses in suburban northern Virginia neighborhoods, where many of the Washington metropolitan area's better public schools are located. Mary Anne would shop for the house, meet with the real-estate people, get a commitment from them to sell the house to us—and then I would show up. After I appeared, some real-estate agents and their clients tried to find ways to wriggle out of the deal. One Arlington agent even counseled a white homeowner to accept a lower offer from a white buyer—and that was in 1985.

But most of the real-estate agents we dealt with in that manner knew they had walked into a trap set by their own racial perceptions, and they were smart enough not to risk a lawsuit.

Unfortunately, my doctors weren't smart enough to consider the possibility that my actual genetic background could lead to my medical undoing, nor did it ever occur to me to bring it up. As it turned out, the initial anti-rejection drugs were too strong for me. They practically wiped out my immune system and unleashed a common virus (polyoma) that attacked the transplanted kidney.

Dr. Gonin was frank but compassionate in conveying the news. Mary Anne's kidney was done in by polyoma, she said. I was losing it. But I already had known that was the case. Everything in my being knew it. I feared climbing stairs, feared doing anything that required more than minimum physical exertion. But I mostly feared telling Mary Anne the truth about my condition and her compromised gift.

I agonized over how to tell her, how to put it into words. At the moment of truth, eloquence yielded to blurting. "I'm losing it," I said after another visit with Dr. Gonin. "She said we should prepare to lose it, and to start dialysis again."

Mary Anne, sitting on the living room sofa where I had spent so many weeks recovering from the initial surgery, was crushed by the news. She buried her head in her hands, shouting "No! No! No!" She believed that God had willed her to give me her kidney. If it was God's will, how could this possibly be happening? "No! No!" she said. "This isn't right. This can't be right. How can this be right?" Mary Anne cried for several days. I cried, too, but never in her presence.

By June 2000, I was back in Georgetown University Hospital in a last-ditch attempt to save Mary Anne's gift. Dr. Gonin was cautiously optimistic. But caution, in this case, meant preparing to return to dialysis—just in case.

I wasn't prepared. I spent much of that year in and out of Georgetown, taking a variety of new drugs, none of which staved off the first transplant's demise. I was getting weak. I tired easily. My feet were swelling grotesquely. Waking up was a chore.

By July 2001, I was back on dialysis. This time, I really hated it. It felt like defeat, failure. I've always hated losing.

Returning to Georgetown on the Potomac to the dialysis laboratory operated by Davita, Inc., was like being sent to the back of the classroom or being held back a grade. It was pure humiliation.

The only good thing about going back, to the extent that there was anything good about it, was seeing Julia Broadus again. Julia was my primary dialysis technician in 1999. She's a bossy, contentious black woman who grew up in the District of Columbia determined to succeed on her own terms.

Working as a dialysis technician was one of Julia's two jobs. She also worked as a prison guard, and often she would come to the dialysis lab only a few hours after leaving guard duty. She acted like it, too. She spoke to patients in the strict voice she used to command inmates. Those of us who loved her laughed at her demeanor, and often we'd do or say things deliberately to provoke her.

I loved her. How could I not? Dialysis techs stick needles in your arms and hook long plastic tubes to catheters imbedded in your chest or neck. It's up close and personal stuff. It's very intimate. You have to trust and believe in the person doing that job. I trusted Julia. She did everything right, and if she really liked you, she did something extra, such as bringing you a pillow (bought with her own money), or a blanket—anything to make you feel comfortable. I got a pillow.

It's always been that way with women and me. I don't know why, but I think it has something to do with the nuns. As a child, I had to learn to understand them in order to get through the day. They seemed to control almost every aspect of my life back then. Figuring out what they would do next, or why they might do it, became a matter of habit. They must've blessed me in return.

All I know is that I'd be dead without women. There was the woman dentist who wouldn't work on me because my blood pressure was too high. There was Dr. Marcus, who forced me to take my condition seriously. There was Mary Anne, who was my first kidney donor, and Dr. Gonin, who strove mightily to save that gift. Women always have been there for me.

Now, women were coming to my aide again. All of the people who volunteered to give me a second kidney transplant were women. Martha turned out to be a match. I didn't ask Martha. She asked me. "You want me to take the tests?" she asked, referring to the medical screening regimen for prospective donors. Just like that. There was no drama, no hesitancy. She offered. I sheepishly said yes. That was that.

Martha's Story

After Warren's first transplant, it was a relief to return to a non-crisis atmosphere. Frank and I still worried about him, but everything seemed to be going well. In the short run, he made frequent visits to the hospital for checkups, but life seemed to be returning to normal for the three of us. We were preoccupied again with stories, with editors, with gossip, with signing up new union members and other daily stuff of newsroom life. It felt good.

Life seemed less troubled than it had been in awhile. I was living happily as a single woman, having spent several years getting to know myself again. If you are married as long as thirty years, particularly if you were married at age nineteen, it's hard to separate the strands of who you are from the choices you made as part of a couple and to know what your individual tastes and enthusiasms are. At least it was for me. Did I use this toothpaste because I liked it best, or had it been Hamilton's brand of choice in which I concurred? It was fun, deciding what to keep and what to throw out.

Meanwhile, our families were doing well. Sarah was still trying to sort out her future and had gone through a difficult period when her dad ran into legal problems. He had been indicted and convicted for being part of an illegal scheme to use Teamster Union dues money to help reelect then-president Ron Carey and had been forced to resign from his job. But she had graduated from college, and, despite her concerns about her dad, she was wonderful, creative, radiant, and on track.

Warren's children also were doing well. Binta was headed toward a career as a high-powered attorney, while Kafi was pursuing a career in journalism. Tony was living with his aunt in New Orleans, where he was being treated like royalty.

Frank's daughters were married or marrying and beginning families of their own.

We kept up with each others' families as if they were part of our own extended network.

When Kafi thought about crossing a picket line during a strike at a television station, Warren thrust the phone at me. "Here. Talk to her," he said.

When Sarah called for car advice, I handed the phone to Frank or Warren.

The three of us kept getting into each other's business in other ways, too. Frank and I kept tabs on Warren's diet. Warren and Frank traded tips on insulin test strips. Frank had been in remission from leukemia since 1986, but had developed diabetes.

Warren wasn't entirely back to normal, but he was close enough to begin treating life, and appointments, casually again. That was worrying because there were continuing problems with his medication. For awhile he was wracked by a terrible parched cough that sounded like something splitting apart. Other times, his hands would shake heavily. Still other times, his gut was so twisted by the medication that he needed a few hours at home in the morning before he could make it into work.

And his eyesight kept changing. Too cheap to get another pair of glasses each time his eyesight changed, Warren kept several pairs on hand and would peer at his computer screen wearing two pairs of glasses at once.

Warren was taking on more work, too. In addition to the column and covering the auto industry, he was working with a publication called *African Americans on Wheels* that runs as a monthly insert in many major metropolitan newspapers, including the *Post*. He also was learning to love life online, doing chats for WashingtonPost.com and starting a weekly online column. Eventually, because being a columnist was taking more and more of his time and attention, he gave up reporting. He was busy and in demand. He was traveling again and feeling footloose. He was doing a regular radio show related to *African Americans on Wheels* and was often interviewed on television and radio.

Frank and I found ways to entertain ourselves when Warren was on the phone pontificating. Warren had acquired a fancy chair with levers that made it go up and down or tilt forward or back. When Warren was on the phone during radio interviews, we rolled our chairs close enough to reach the levers with our toes. The game was to see how Warren kept his composure as his chair shot up and down or flipped forward or back.

The doctors had predicted that Mary Anne's kidney would be good for at least five to eight years, and Warren was determined to get the most out of those years professionally before he had to return to dialysis, die, or plan on another transplant.

But he still wasn't facing how his illness had transformed his life. Before the transplant, he had either ignored or minimized his health problems. At his most serious, he would treat them as a passing problem—something that ultimately would be solved. The transplant had seemed to vindicate that attitude. In Warren's mind, he was over it. His problems were in the past.

But they weren't.

During the summer of 2000, there were signs that things were going wrong. Warren was weak and anemic. We watched his panic grow deeper and deeper as he came to terms with the fact that Mary Anne's kidney was failing. In June, Warren went in for additional tests. He drove a Mercedes roadster with a stick shift, anticipating that he would be tested and go home.

But the doctors wouldn't let him go home. They kept him there to start chemotherapy through an intravenous drip in a last-ditch attempt to save his kidney. Mary Anne couldn't drive stick shift, so Warren called Frank to drive Mary Anne home.

When Frank arrived, Warren was being Warren. "Everything is fine," he told Frank.

Warren was sitting on the bed with his computer, writing, trying to maintain the appearance of normalcy with three shunts in his neck and another line into his arm. But when Frank and Mary Anne walked down the hall away from the room, Mary Anne dissolved in tears. "Frank, he's not all right," she said between her sobs.

In the car, Frank ran into a problem shifting into reverse. "Here's what we're going to do," he said. "We're either going to sit here until the car in front of us moves or until I get it into reverse," he said. "I'm a guy, and guys don't ask for directions. I'm not going to go in there and ask how to get it in reverse." Mary Anne laughed.

"What does Warren do?" Frank asked. Mary Anne said she thought she remembered that he pulled up on the collar around the gearshift. That worked. Frank drove Mary Anne to the house, where she picked up clothes so she could sleep in Warren's hospital room, as she always did, unwilling to let him out of her sight when he was in danger.

—————

Warren was slow to admit how bad things were. We grilled him constantly, but he downplayed what he didn't want to acknowledge. At first it was, "Well, they think there is a problem with the kidney." Then it was, "They say I may need another transplant sooner than they thought." Then it was, "They want to put me on dialysis to get ready for another transplant."

He couldn't bring himself to tell us that his health was failing, and failing fast.

But the signs were there. He was looking unhealthy again. His ankles had swollen to elephant-like proportions. He fell asleep in the middle of phone conversations. We tried to keep it light. "Hey, it's Warren 'Fat Foot' Brown," we'd say when he walked in with his ankles thickened with fluid.

But when Warren wasn't around, we talked to each other about how sick and how frightened he had become.

I offered again to be tested to see if I was a potential kidney donor. But when another friend of Warren's beat me to the punch, that was fine with me.

Warren's friend Lydia Bendersky started the regime of tests to establish whether she was a potential donor. The first results looked good.

After weeks of testing, Warren was counting on the surgery, and his fear was lifting. It would be two weeks, three

at the most. He was scheduling activities around the anticipated surgery date, planning to write columns in advance
for the weeks he would be laid up. He was lighthearted
again.

And then it fell apart.

Frank and I had headed up to Capitol Hill in the early
afternoon on an errand. In the cab we were talking to each
other about looking forward to getting through the next
round of surgery. But when we returned to the newsroom a
few hours later, Warren was downcast. His friend couldn't be
a donor. There was a problem with platelets not matching.

"Hey, no biggie," said Warren. But I had never seen him
so stricken.

"You want me to take the tests?" I asked. I couldn't have
kept from saying it.

[7]

Waiting

Martha's Story

"Who do I call?"

Warren scribbled the name and number of a transplant coordinator at Georgetown on a sheet of notebook paper and pushed it across the desk with a note: "Blood type needed is B or O."

I knew when I offered that blood type wouldn't be a problem. I'm O negative, the universal blood donor. I've donated blood since I was twenty, when I lied about my age and weight at a hospital in Buenos Aires to donate blood for a friend's aunt.

I called the number instantly and left my name and number, slightly impatient that the transplantation coordinator wasn't immediately available. Having taken the first step, I wanted to move; I wanted the process to be under way. But the organ donation process is designed to weed out the ill-thought decision, and it isn't fast.

First there was the back-and-forth over whether I or another volunteer would be tested first. Then, transplant coordinator Alvanetta Cribbs called back and began to run through a questionnaire about my suitability as a donor. "Mmmmm. That might be a problem," she said at one point as we went through a series of questions about my health and habits over the phone. I was answering as discreetly as I could sitting in the newsroom between Frank and Warren, who were, of course, listening intently.

But there were no problems in my medical history, and by September 5, I had my official-looking laminated blue "transplant donor card" and the first of a series of schedules for the medical procedures that would determine whether I was a suitable donor.

In the months that followed, I would live with a mixture of doubt and determination. In a heartbeat, I would swing from wanting to be instantly on the operating table to wondering if I was doing something stupid. But while I might have my own occasional misgivings, any suggestion that I might not qualify or that my kidney might not work stung me into a greater determination than ever to succeed.

Oddly, I worried more about what people would think than about the operation itself. I didn't want the word to get out in the newsroom, a place where everyone speculates about everyone else's motives. I knew becoming a donor for Warren would trigger questions, including inevitable speculation about the nature of our relationship or whether this was some weird act of liberal guilt. And I underestimated the kindness and support that turned out to be the more universal reaction. So I told Warren and Frank to keep it quiet.

The decision made perfect sense to me, but not everyone shared my perspective. I'd been through years of watching Warren close up as his health deteriorated. I'd seen the joy after the first transplant give way to fear and disappointment. I'd watched fatigue and despair set in, as they will when people are very sick for a long time. And I knew that Warren had always been there to help me when I needed it.

If I had been younger or had children at home, I probably wouldn't have offered. But at age fifty-five, with no family history of kidney disease, and a grandmother, aunt, and mother who have lived into their late eighties or early nineties, I felt I had nothing to fear.

Of course, there were people inside and outside the newsroom whom I had to tell. I told my mother, my daughter Sarah, and my sister JE, and I told Jill Dutt, the head of financial news. Everyone was supportive, though my mother clearly was worried. "I like Warren and want him to do well," she said. "But you're my daughter."

My daughter Sarah said: "Tell Warren I'll give him a kidney."

My sister JE was supportive, but I knew my hospitalization—if it came to that—would be hard on her. She had gone through so many hospitalizations with her husband Rick before he died in 1993, and those memories would come flooding back.

As the tests began, so did the frustration of dealing with the hospital, a large organization in which employees tend to small pieces of the process, often without sharing information. The blood letting, urine vetting, interviews, EKGs, X rays, and Magnetic Resonance Imaging test (MRI), which required spending an hour lying nearly motionless in a metal tube, weren't vexing. But the small things were—especially the breakdown in lines of communication. I would arrive at the lab for blood tests, only to be required to repeat information I had given on my previous visit just days before. The information went into a computer, from which I can only assume it disappeared, since I'd be asked for the same information the next time I came. My blood pressure and temperature would be taken in one room and entered into the computer, then taken again in another room ten minutes later and entered again in some vast information dump where no one ever looked.

The hospital's mix-ups on appointments and billing were even more unnerving. I needed to feel confident about the hospital where I was headed for slicing and dicing, and those errors didn't inspire confidence.

In the meantime, Warren and I were in an awkward place—for two reasons. First, we weren't supposed to deal directly with each other about the transplant. His transplant coordinator was supposed to talk to my transplant coordinator to minimize any chance that Warren would be able to coerce me into doing something against my will—as if he could. But, hey, it was Warren and me—sitting next to each other, keeping a watchful eye on each other, and mutually concerned that it would work.

Unspoken but even more awkward was that the kidney transplant would be a new kind of intimacy between us, a strange joining together of two lives beyond the normal bounds of our friendship. We were close, yes, but that closeness had its limits, and this would go beyond them. We dealt with that awkwardness by ignoring it.

And, oh, yeah, there was work. I was covering the retail beat, and the calendar was approaching the most critical months of the retail year, the holiday season.

Then, six days after I received my organ donor card, the terror attacks of September 11 occurred—simultaneously making me feel petty about my own anxieties and adding to them.

Like so many others on the East Coast that day, I'd been delighting in the perfect, beautiful late summer morning. It was so beautiful, I didn't even turn on the radio to catch the news. I poured a cup of coffee and headed out to the back porch to enjoy the weather.

I had friends visiting, Tracy and Dick Guy, the parents of Sarah's long-time best friend Nicole Guy (Nikki). They had moved earlier in the year from D.C. to St. Croix for their retirement. But they were back in town for doctors' appointments. Tracy and I were drinking coffee and chatting on the porch when Dick came downstairs. "Did you hear anything about a plane hitting the World Trade Towers?" he asked. He had just heard a report on the radio. We turned on the television and began watching the awful news.

Within minutes, the phone rang. It was Nikki, sobbing and hysterical. Nikki is a flight attendant with Delta, based in Manhattan. The news had hit close to home for her.

As soon as Dick got off the phone I grabbed it and called Sarah, who was sound asleep in the pre-dawn hours on the West Coast. "This isn't about anybody in your family," I said, knowing that would be her instant fear about an early morning phone call. "But you need to know this." Afterward, I dressed quickly to go to work. Driving the ten minutes downtown, listening to the radio, I heard the news as the second tower collapsed and the Pentagon was hit. Everyone had rushed into the newsroom in a combination of professionalism, instinct, and a deep-seated desire to be where the action was. There was said to be a fourth plane in the air, but no one thought about leaving, despite our proximity to the White House, another potential target.

Don Phillips, who covers airline crashes, was on the phone on what would become an all-day phone call, holding and waiting for whatever bits of information the Federal Aviation Administration could pass along. Another reporter, Caroline Mayer, and I took over, staying on hold and taking intermittent notes, so that Don would be free to chase other sources.

In between, I called the Federal Bureau of Prisons (BOP). My ex-husband Hamilton was being held in the Metropolitan Corrections Center in downtown Manhattan, not far from the site of the attack. Former Teamsters Union president Ron Carey was on trial, and Hamilton was a witness. Carey was later acquitted.

Hamilton had been in prison since April 2001, serving time in a minimum security facility in Cumberland, Maryland. Sarah and her brother Mark, my stepson, had been supportive of their dad throughout the process, but it was hard on them. Sarah came to Washington to spend time with her dad before Hamilton reported to prison.

To his credit, Hamilton spent lots of time with Sarah that week, even driving her out to Cumberland, which seemed to help allay her worst fears about where he would be spending his time.

In Sarah's view, Hamilton was in prison for standing up for what he believed in, including Ron Carey and his leadership of the Teamsters. So she wasn't stricken by his imprisonment. But she did worry about him in general and was even more worried now, knowing that he was near the scene of the attack.

She called right after I'd talked to the BOP, and I was able to tell her that the corrections center was undamaged. Then I called Mark and my ex-in-laws to tell them. "You're a good, good, good, good, good girl," said Weir Hamilton, my ex-father-in-law.

In the newsroom everyone was on the phones calling any sources they had. It was an oddly reassuring place to be, with Warren and Frank by my side.

Two days later I was at Georgetown for more blood tests, an EKG, and a chest X-ray. The televisions were on in all the waiting rooms, full of follow-up on the terrorist attacks. No one spoke to anyone except when they had to. We were transfixed.

In the face of so much death and destruction, it seemed almost pointless to be giving a kidney to help keep one person alive, I thought, as I watched along with the rest of the waiting room. But it's not meaningless to Warren, I reminded myself. It wasn't meaningless to Mary Anne, Tony, Binta, and Kafi. And it wasn't meaningless to Warren's many friends, I thought, of whom I am one.

I was beginning to understand a little more about what to expect in the operation. I took advantage of the Guys' visit to pump them with questions. Dick is a doctor, an obstetrician-gynecologist, and Tracy is a nurse. Why did they need to make four incisions to take out the kidney? It wasn't clear reading the materials Georgetown had provided.

One incision was for the camera, Dick explained. Two more were for the chopsticks or whatever they use to do the pruning. The fourth, the slightly larger one, was the one through which the kidney would be removed. Dick mentioned that they blow your abdomen full of gas so they have room to maneuver. That's something I had forgotten, although Warren had talked about how that was the source of the worst discomfort to Mary Anne after the operation. Dick also described how other instruments would siphon off blood and suction away smoke. Generated in the cutting, I think he said. Somehow, Dick's description made the operation more vivid than the literature. It was a useful reality check, but not enough to change my mind.

I spent that morning two days after the attack at Georgetown, being tested, and then went back to work. I was working with Frank now on stories about the airline industry. We were busy working on a beat we'd both covered for years, finding comfort in the work and our easy partnership. We were expecting Warren later in the day, but he didn't make it. Dialysis that day had dropped his blood pressure lower than it should have been, leaving him disabled. Dialysis was getting harder and harder on Warren. Once he had been able to laugh it off as "a lube job" or "an oil change" and to stick to something close to a normal schedule. Now the treatment increasingly left him weak and wiped out.

As unsettling as the events were that led to it, working on a major breaking story was a godsend and a pain reliever, a distraction from my personal worries as well as a way to deal with the national horror. I worked straight through to Saturday and would have worked Sunday gladly, but they didn't need me. By then the Guys had driven to New York to see Nikki, so I was home alone. I spent the day keeping busy. I did yard work and then headed over to my vegetable garden in a park a few blocks away.

None of the other gardeners were around that day, and there were only a few dog walkers in the park. The Sunday soccer games appeared to have been canceled.

It was the height of the growing season, and there was plenty to do, so I worked steadily for about two hours. Finally, dripping with sweat and hungry, I picked up my bags of ripe tomatoes, okra, butter beans, peppers, and flowers and straightened up, ready to leave. And I suddenly noticed the park was empty.

I panicked. I was sure some other horror had unfolded while I was gardening. I rushed to the car and turned on the radio, but there was no major new news. By then I was trembling.

So I went home, showered, and had brunch. I walked up to the neighborhood bookstore, Politics & Prose. Owner Carla Cohen was sitting on a bench in front of the store, taking a break. Books on Islam were flying out of the store, she said, as we sat and shook our heads over the week's events. Then I went home and did more yard work. I was having a hard time being alone. By the time the Guys called early in the evening to say they were driving back from New York and wanted to stay at the house, I was a mess. When they arrived a few hours later with Nikki, whom I could hug as a surrogate for Sarah, I was incredibly relieved.

During the day, besides fighting off panic with busy work, I had one other chore—a twenty-four-hour urine test. That meant peeing into an orange plastic bottle and keeping it refrigerated. It's just as well that I hadn't had to work that day, I thought, since I didn't think my coworkers would have welcomed the bottle of urine in the tiny refrigerator where we keep our lunches.

I had excellent urine, according to the test, and every other test also turned out well. In addition to the tests there was a series of interviews in the final week of September. I was checked out by a nephrologist, a psychiatrist, and a social worker and judged fit.

While Warren and I took turns visiting Georgetown, we were also working on another project. Frank had turned sixty-five earlier in September. Warren and I had planned all along to do something special to celebrate, but we put our plans on hold after the attack. Then we regrouped. "Some things are still worth celebrating," we said on the invitation to the surprise party (the more surprising because it would occur many days after his birthday). "Our friend Frank's 65th birthday is one of them."

The Business section writers and editors and others who had worked in the section over the years cheerfully and conspiratorially helped plan the party at my house. Warren wasn't feeling well, so I knew I would have to do most of the work, helped by Caroline and others. But Warren's role was key. He was in charge of getting Frank to my house.

Warren's ruse was genius. He told Frank that Bill Ford, the chairman of Ford Motor Co., wanted to get together briefly on Saturday night. What he hadn't counted on was that Frank had agreed to baby-sit his grandchildren and was prepared to choose baby-sitting over Bill Ford. So Warren improvised. He convinced Frank that he had moved the meeting up, and that Frank could meet with Ford and be home in time to baby-sit. His baby-sitting was part of the ruse.

Warren's finest touch was to have Mike Moran, one of Ford Motor Company's Washington representatives, call Frank to chat with him about the interview. Frank was completely taken in. On September 29, Warren picked up Frank at home and headed to D.C., mentioning that he had to drop medical records by my house. When Frank walked in, he was clueless—until the crowd crouched in my kitchen jumped up. "I've always referred to myself as a veteran observer," he said later that night. "I guess I'm going to have to drop the 'observer' part." It was our best gotcha.

The party was a huge success. Planning it was a pleasure because everyone loves Frank and everyone wanted to help. And it was an opportunity for Warren and me to acknowledge publicly how much Frank meant to us. We knew he planned on retiring a few months later and leaving the Elder Pod. We knew there would be *Post* celebrations for Frank then. But this was our personal celebration.

Days later, on October 1, we appeared to be, finally, on

the verge of an operation. I came home to find a message on my telephone from Ms. Cribbs saying that the surgery could be done on October 16. I called Warren, who said that was fine with him. He hadn't been at work because he had come down with an infection where they inserted the catheter for dialysis.

Immediately I began making plans around the date. I told JE that she and Frank would need to organize my postsurgical care. I didn't have the energy to do it myself. I told my mother and Sarah and other family and friends. Sarah suggested that Frank should have his appendix out in solidarity.

And then, three days later, the operation was off.

I came home on October 3 to find another message from Ms. Cribbs. The surgery on October 16 had been canceled because Warren needed more tests. I called Warren, who said no, no, no—that he had done all the tests. But later he called and left a different message: He needed to finish a course of antibiotics, and then he'd get a biopsy to see if he still had the virus had destroyed Mary Anne's kidney.

I was furious at Warren. I had been organizing my life around a surgery date of October 16, without a clue from Warren—who knew or should have known—that the surgery might have to be postponed. I spent much of the day calling and e-mailing folks to tell them that the surgery had been put off.

During the planning for the party, Warren had promised to do a few small things besides luring Frank to my house, and on most of them, he hadn't delivered, prompting me to joke that I alternated between not wanting Warren to die and wanting to kill him.

Now it wasn't funny any more and I was coming down hard on the side of killing him. I didn't know whether Warren had been aware of the need for a biopsy and had shut it out of his mind or what, but he wasn't giving me information that I needed. I felt abused and treated like a fool instead of a friend. It wasn't rational. It was angry, and it was a good thing that Warren wasn't in the newsroom the morning after I found out.

By the time he arrived later in the day, my anger had subsided. He said that he and another dialysis patent, both attended by the same technician, had *E. coli* infections. Warren had been put on a twenty-one-day course of antibiotics to clear up the infection, and he would need a blood test at the end of the treatment to make sure the infection had disappeared. The infection was around the catheter in his shoulder that the dialysis center used for hosing his blood in and out of his body. The biopsy was to make sure that the virus that killed Mary Anne's kidney was gone. I was reminded again how sick Warren was, and I felt like a jerk.

———

As it turned out, the postponement was a good thing. I hadn't focused on the fact that October 16 was the anniversary of my brother-in-law Rick's death from kidney failure, among other things. JE hadn't reminded me, but it would have been inhumanely hard on her to have spent that particular day in a hospital. My nephew Russell was only eight when his dad died, and now he was turning sixteen. For JE, it was another sadness to think that Russell had lived longer now without his dad than with him. In my preoccupation with my own impending surgery, I hadn't realized how much she was hurting.

And as for the delay, it was tougher on Warren, who had to spend more time on the debilitating dialysis, than on me.

It wasn't only my waking hours that were consumed by the prospect of the transplant. My dreams were filled with images—unsubtle, heavy-handed images—of what lay ahead. In one I dreamed I was transplanting a rosebush and worried about whether it would thrive in the new location. In another, I was planting a seed bed by making a slit in my skin into which to tuck the seeds. And, as I cut, it hurt.

So we settled in for the delay.

A few weeks later, Warren sent a message saying he was going to Georgetown for some outpatient checks. When he arrived in the newsroom, he had a date for the biopsy but hadn't asked how soon thereafter we might do the surgery.

"Warren," I said wearily, "you've got to find out about that sort of thing so I can plan."

In one area, I decided I needed to do some reporting myself. Warren had told me a little about the virus that destroyed Mary Anne's kidney, the polyoma virus. It exists in almost everyone's body, but our normal immune systems keep it in check. Warren's normal immune system had been wiped out by the anti-rejection drugs, which allowed the virus to flourish and kill Mary Anne's kidney.

If that could happen to Mary Anne's kidney, could it happen to mine? What I found was reassuring. There didn't appear to be much research on the issue, but what there was looked good. One study found that out of eight patients who had received a subsequent kidney after losing the first transplant to polyoma, only one had lost the second kidney. Those seemed like good odds to me. And the National Institutes of Health was interested in the polyoma virus and planning to keep tabs on Warren after the surgery, so I felt confident there would be close monitoring.

I was beginning to realize that Warren's failure to pursue the details that I thought I needed to know probably stemmed from his fatigue with the whole process. He had been sick for a long time now. On top of that, he was limited in what he could do professionally at a time when opportunities were springing up. Just getting through the day was tough enough, and being the rock on which his family depended must have been far harder. Not that we talked about it. Warren's general pose in life is that of the lighthearted guy, the funny, breezy friend whose most frequent answer to any problem is "Not to worry. . . ." So, despite my occasional carping at Warren, we usually kept it light, with Frank and me supplying the kidney jokes as often as Warren.

As I went through my own rounds of testing and interviewing, I realized that I also was not pursuing information as hard as I might have as a reporter. For instance, I realized only after the fact that I should have asked what kinds of complications donors have had and what the implications might be for insurance rates if I were to change jobs. (The complications are relatively minor, and donating a kidney doesn't appear to have an impact on health-insurance rates, I later found out.)

I had been similarly unprobing the first time I had surgery when I was in my twenties. I had breezed into the hospital expecting to go home right after the surgery, which was being done under local anesthetic. I hadn't asked Hamilton, who was working in Washington while I was living and going to school in Austin, to come down.

Even when the hospital staff questioned why I didn't bring an overnight bag, I brushed it off. I watched the surgery in a reflective light fixture over the table as my doctor, who was assisting the surgeon, explained the fine points of removing what turned out to be a fibrous cyst from my breast.

It was only after the anesthetic began wearing off that I realized that I might have had to decide whether to have a breast removed, and that—holy hell!—it hurts when they slice open your skin. I spent the night in the hospital taking liberal doses of pain killers.

As we continued to wait for a date with the surgeons, life—and death—went on. It had been a sad year at the *Post* because of the death in July of publisher Katharine Graham. And now it became a sadder year with the death in October of Herb Block, the editorial cartoonist. Herb's health, but never his wit, had been failing for some time. The last time I had seen him had been at Mrs. Graham's funeral, which he attended in a wheelchair. It was clear, when no "Herblock" cartoons appeared after September 11, that Herb must be very sick.

Everyone at the *Post* loved and revered Herb, a brilliantly caustic and sweet-natured man. Herb and Frank had become close over the years. Frank was one of a handful of people Herb would ask to look at the four or five cartoons he was working on to help him choose the strongest for the next day. I would turn away while they consorted. But on infrequent lucky days, Herb would pass the cartoons to me as well and say: "Let's see how Mikey likes it."

Frank was honored to have been named by Herb as an honorary pallbearer. What he didn't know at the time was that Herb also had named him to the board of directors of the Herb Block Foundation, which would later lead to a new job for Frank as president of the foundation.

I knew Warren would be driving to the cathedral for Herb's funeral, so I asked him for a ride. During the service, Warren fell asleep a couple of times, as he had in the days before his first transplant when he was very ill. Afterward, Warren gave Frank a ride back to the office, too. When Warren was away from his desk, I told Frank about the nodding off, so we could both worry about Warren, who was looking worse as every day went by.

Two months had passed, and at the end of October we still didn't know when the transplant would occur. One of Frank's jobs at the *Post* was editing the car pages and Warren's automotive reviews. For months, he had been pressing Warren to write reviews in advance of the surgery. Now, with Warren often too exhausted by dialysis sometimes to write, Frank encouraged him just to test drive without worrying about writing. If he made notes on his test drives, he would be able to dictate reviews after the operation. But he wrote anyway.

I had my own professional concerns. By now it was clear the operation would be bumping up against Thanksgiving, the busiest time of the year for the retail beat, my beat, so I suggested moving someone else onto the beat since I probably wouldn't be around. I would be away from work recovering during most of the holiday shopping season, so it made sense to get someone else covering retail as quickly as possible. I felt responsible for the beat, so I felt better once plans were under way to have my colleague Dina ElBoghdady begin to take over coverage.

I began doing some reporting on another issue. Warren's bout with the polyoma virus had raised questions about race and ethnicity, since his regime of immunosuppressant drugs was based on his self-identification as black. We had joked about race-mixing and how we might be kinfolk since we came from the same part of the country. I began to think about how little I knew about my own family. As Warren began questioning kinfolk and looking into his own heritage, I also became more interested in mine.

My family is working-class southern out of Scotland on both sides, but beyond that I didn't know very much. I knew my daddy's father died when Daddy was ten, and that he and his siblings were farmed out to various relatives, with Daddy ending up in DeQuincey, Louisiana. I thought my paternal granddad, a machinist who worked in a textile mill in Georgia, was originally from Scotland, but that turned out to be wrong. It was my great-grandfather who had immigrated.

I knew more about my mother's side as a result of growing up surrounded by her family, but my memories were vague. So I started asking my mother about what I thought I remembered, and some of the answers I got were disturbing. I had grown up hearing vague mutterings about a Senator Bilbo. Bilbo was my great-grandmother's maiden name, and she came from Mississippi. Her story, my mother said, was that there were two branches of the Bilbo family, ours and the senator's. I had the impression that Bilbo was scandalous, but I didn't realize till I looked it up how loathsome he was. Senator Theodore Bilbo, the author of *Take Your Choice: Separation or Mongrelization* (1947), was not just a liar and philanderer. He was so egregiously racist that the U.S. Senate refused to seat him in 1947. I thank my great-grandmother for taking the pains to distinguish our family from his.

And while my mother was explaining this history, I discovered something else I didn't know about my family. We had owned slaves. I had always assumed that, because my family was working class, we were exempt from that stain. But we weren't. The family of my great-grandfather Joseph Hill Humphrey, husband of the former Virginia Bilbo, owned two or three slaves, including one who grew up with my great-grandfather and was his "body servant."

They stayed close even after Emancipation, according to my mother, and when my great-grandfather died, the former slave attended the funeral and wept over my grandfather's death, according to what my mother had been told.

Well, it was a slight shift in my view of myself to realize that some of my relatives had been slave owners. We know so little about ourselves, given our own and our forebears' delusions. But, whatever the past, I am who I am.

At one point Warren and I thought we might have genetic material in common, but it turned out that the chromosomal trait we shared meant no more than sharing a blood type. Even so, we felt a kinship created over the years at the *Washington Post*.

Finally, after all the frustration and uncertainty, we had a date for the surgery—November 20. Anxiety over not knowing when it would happen gave way to anxiety over knowing. We had fifteen days' notice.

The surgery was set for the Tuesday before Thanksgiving. Frank started making jokes about carving up turkeys. Sarah sent me an e-mail warning me to look out for anthrax, terrorists, and Frank's sense of humor. And Warren and I both began planning in earnest for the operation and recuperation. By now the news of the operation was widespread within the newsroom. It was hard to know what to say when colleagues would come up and offer support, often with a friendly squeeze of the arm or a pat on the back. I told Frank to tell people who asked what to say to please tell them not to say how brave I am, a remark that invariably made me wonder if I underestimated what I was getting into. Frank told me to work on my graciousness.

Finally I hit on what seemed to be the right formula: "Thank you," I would say. "That's nice of you to say."

Warren and I had agreed to write about the transplant operation for the *Post*'s Health section. Our colleague Susan Okie, a doctor as well as a reporter, had gotten permission to be in the operating rooms to describe the surgery, accompanied by photographer Michael Williamson. Sarah was scheduled to arrive the night before the surgery. I was beginning to feel cheerful, looking forward to having it over and done with. That didn't mean that the occasional doubt didn't still creep in at 4 in the morning when the jet fighters and helicopters patrolling overhead made it hard to sleep.

Ten days before the operation, I was riding with my sister, my mother, and my nephew up Rockville Pike in Maryland on our way to lunch. We passed a guy on the median strip. The shunt in his shoulder was visible in the stretched-out neck of the white cotton T-shirt he wore. He held a hand-lettered sign that said, "Homeless. On dialysis. Can't work."

"I should roll down the window," I said, "and tell him—'I gave at the office.'"

Warren's Story

The year 2001 wasn't a good one for Mary Anne. Her mother, Omadel Fowler-Reed, died in January after a long illness. She and Mary Anne, along with one of Mary Anne's sisters, Joan George, were best friends. The three of them would talk for hours on the phone—Virginia to Texas. Sometimes, it drove me crazy thinking about the cost of those calls. Other times, I laughed. Their ability to sustain endless conversation amused me.

Ma Reed actually left the trio before her death. She became senile. Occasionally, her once sharp wit would cut through the descending veil. But, more often than not, she drifted on a sea of amnesia, unable to remember names or places. Mary Anne and Joan understood, but they were saddened by their mother's frequent inability to remember their names.

The phone chatter reflected their disappointment.

"Does she remember you and Tanya?" Mary Anne asked in one of those talks. Tanya, Mary Anne and Joan's older sister, lives in Dallas.

"Does she remember Bill?" Mary Anne asked, referring to one of her brothers. She went through a list of family names. "I hope she remembers me," Mary Anne said.

Tears often stained those conversations. Sometimes, there was laughter. But the phone talk usually resumed its solemn tone, as it did on one occasion, when it turned toward me.

Mary Anne's voice dropped to a whisper. "Well, he's not doing so well since he went back on dialysis," she said. Pause. "I don't know," she continued. "He's tired all the time...."

"He has several offers," Mary Anne continued. "They're all women. Maybe Lydia, maybe Martha.... I don't know."

I pretended not to listen. Listening would have meant talking about it after Mary Anne finished with Joan. Talking about it usually ended with Mary Anne in tears. It was hard to console her.

"I feel like I failed you," she said in one crying episode. "I feel like I failed everybody." I told her that she wasn't God. It wasn't her fault that the first anti-rejection therapy didn't work. Nor was it her fault that Ma Reed died. I could have died, had she not given me use of a good kidney for nearly a year.

"You gave me a year off dialysis," I said to Mary Anne. "You gave me at least another year of life. Maybe that was all I needed to get to this point."

———

I reminded her that she was the religious one in the family, the one who never, ever missed Mass, or skipped services on Holy Days of Obligation. She was the one who went to Holy Communion every Sunday, who prayed every night. I was the one hanging onto her spiritual coattails, hoping that God would overlook my transgressions and allow me to become a saint by association.

"Where is your faith, Mary Anne?" I asked. "You're the one who's more Catholic than the Pope. Where is your faith?"

That only made her angry.

"You don't understand!" she shouted. "I'm your wife. I wanted to save you. I wanted you to have my kidney. I gave you my kidney, and now it's all ruined." More crying.

The best way to stop Mary Anne from crying is to really piss her off. I could deal with her anger better than her tears.

"So," I said. "This is about ego? You would rather I die than have another woman's kidney?"

"You're an ass!" she shouted, dry-eyed. I smiled, which made her angrier.

"Why haven't any men offered you a kidney?" she asked.

"How the hell am I supposed to know that?" I responded.

"I don't get it," Mary Anne said. "All of these women offering you kidneys. Where are the men?"

———

"Should I wait for a man to make an offer? I could be dead by then," I said. I truly believed that. Men are not nearly as generous as women. That has been my life's experience.

"I only wish that my kidney had worked. I wanted you to have my kidney," Mary Anne said. I could say nothing to that.

In August, I learned that my friend Lydia Bendersky was not a match. I tried to shrug it off, but couldn't. I have certain ideas about organ donations. My donor has to be a spiritual as well as a biological match. I'm not talking about religion. Spirituality, here, concerns the quality of soul.

Lydia is a Chilean Jew. I'm a black Roman Catholic. No matter. Lydia has a good soul. She'd give her last nickel if she thought that giving it would do the world some good. I didn't ask her to take medical tests to determine if she would be a suitable donor. She volunteered. "I have two. You need one," she said. Where had I heard that before? Martha, of course. "I have two good kidneys. You need one...."

I figure that if you're going to be that intimate with someone—sharing body parts—you'd better know something about the person. You'd better know if she's good or evil, a hater or a lover. I'm serious. It's a karma thing. It's why I was not of a mind to receive a kidney, be it from a living or dead donor, from someone I never knew. To me, taking a part of that person into my body would have been the same as accepting a part of that person's spirit.

I didn't need bad karma from someone else. I generated enough of that on my own.

Lydia didn't work out. Tests showed that our antibodies were naturally hostile toward one another. That would've been bad for a kidney transplant, or a transplant of any sort. The news depressed me, but it seemed to depress Lydia even more.

"I wanted to help," she said.

Lydia proposed giving one of her kidneys to someone else, solely as a way of moving me up on the list of patients awaiting organs from deceased donors. The donor system works that way. If someone donates an organ to someone else in your name, you move up on the list of prospective organ recipients.

But I couldn't ask Lydia to make a donation to another person just to help me. I asked her to reconsider. She did, but she kept the offer open in case I changed my mind. I didn't. I resigned myself to a longer stay on dialysis, even though Martha earlier had made a standing offer to give me a kidney. I didn't think I had the right to ask Martha to follow through. As it turned out, I didn't have to ask her at all. "I have two good kidneys. You need one." She volunteered.

———

I had hope again. But then the unthinkable happened. September 11. I'd fallen asleep moments after the technician hooked my chest catheter to the dialysis machine. Sleeping in the dialysis lab was my way of escaping the reality of where I was at the moment. But I usually slept only when my regular technician, Julia Broadus, was attending to my needs. Julia wasn't there September 11, but I was tired and slept anyway.

That was taking a chance. I had a substitute dialysis technician, and substitutes always made me nervous. I didn't know them and they didn't know me. I knew nothing about their training, or lack of it, and the only thing they knew about me was what they thought they read on my medical charts. Dialysis under that circumstance calls for patient vigilance, not sleep. But I nodded off.

Often when I've wound up seriously dehydrated after a dialysis session, it was because a substitute technician took too much fluid out of my system. Almost always when anything went wrong with me in dialysis, a substitute had something to do with it.

I believe that is how I contracted a painful *E. coli* infection—either through my catheter, or through the opening in my chest where the catheter was inserted. I know that a patient who normally sits across from me had an *E. coli* infection several days before I came down with it. I know that a substitute dialysis technician was serving both of us when the fellow across from me fell ill. I know that Julia wasn't handling my dialysis at the time.

Had Julia been there, I believe I would not have gotten the *E. coli* bug. The woman was fastidious in patient care. She did it by the books—washing hands, changing gloves, avoiding contact with contaminants. I trusted her.

But I was too tired to worry about Julia's absence on September 11. I'd stayed up too late the night before working on a column. I slept until a chorus of exclamations awakened me.

Each of the patient chairs in the lab at Georgetown on the Potomac is adjacent to a small, overhead television. Patients and techs alike were glued to those TVs that tragic morning. I turned on my overhead set. "Oh, my God!" I said repeatedly. "A jet crashed into the World Trade Center? How could that be?"

My thoughts turned to Binta and Kafi, my New York daughters. Kafi was living on the Upper West Side near Columbia University, where she was a graduate journalism student. She was well away from the Trade Center. But Binta, a lawyer now, was working near the area. She often met with clients and friends there.

I tried reaching both of them by cell phone, a useless endeavor. I panicked. But the girls already had called Mary

Anne at Glebe Elementary School in Arlington where she teaches fifth grade. Mary Anne called me. The girls were okay, she said. But Mary Anne wasn't okay. There were tears and panic in her voice. She'd gone through hell before she got those calls from Binta and Kafi.

I thought about Frank and Martha—and bylines. This was a big story. Everyone would be working on it. Both Martha and Frank had covered the airlines. Surely, they would be called in on this story. Tired or not, I didn't want to be left out. I wanted to get to the office as quickly as possible. I asked the substitute tech to take me off the dialysis machine an hour earlier. He easily complied. Had Julia been there, she would have given me hell in the form of a lecture about "acting against medical advice."

Another plane crashed into the second tower. Suddenly, I was happy that Julia wasn't on duty. I can't manipulate her. But the substitute tech was a pushover. He disconnected me. I went to the office, where, as expected, I found Frank and Martha hustling on the airline part of the story. I joined them.

A month later, Mary Anne and I, accompanied by our daughter Binta, went to the National Institutes of Health in Bethesda, Maryland, where we met with Dr. Jeffrey B. Kopp, senior investigator in the institute's kidney disease section. Dr. Gonin, my nephrologist at Georgetown, had arranged the visit.

Dr. Kopp was studying how the polyoma virus had been set loose to attack my first kidney transplant. He wanted to know how and why the virus goes on the warpath in certain kidney transplant patients, and how it responds to certain immunosuppressant drugs.

It wasn't going to be an easy visit. Mary Anne is an absolute pain when she wants to know something, and she was determined to find out why her kidney died in me. Binta was in a third-degree mood, too. I was torn between wanting to leave and wanting to stay and hear what Dr. Kopp had to say.

I stayed, of course. But, as I feared would be the case, my physical examination at NIH was much shorter than the Mary Anne/Binta Quiz Show. Luckily, Dr. Kopp, an affable and knowledgeable man, was up to the task.

Dr. Kopp said the polyoma virus was as common as dirt. It could have been in Mary Anne's kidney. Maybe not. I could've had it all along. Maybe not. The point is that nearly everybody has it. It's a relatively harmless virus in most people. But in people with suppressed immune systems, it can cause problems.

Dr. Kopp's comments made me wonder if it was worth it, or ethically right, to accept Martha's tendered gift. What if the polyoma virus came back? I didn't want Martha's donation to go the same route as Mary Anne's. It's one thing for me to deal with dialysis. It's another to ask a friend to suffer in vain.

Dr. Kopp, in that way that doctors say things without saying anything definite, said that there was every chance that the polyoma virus was removed from my system, or made dormant by the combination of dialysis and the discontinuation of immunosuppressant drugs. He said most patients who lost one transplant to the virus tended not to lose a second one the same way. He made me feel better.

Dr. Kopp said that my initial anti-rejection drug therapy might have been too aggressive, so much so that it wiped out my immune system, thereby turning a relatively harmless virus into a destructive force. Some doctors at Georgetown had suggested the same thing earlier, though no one knew anything for sure.

But there was a buzz going on in the medical community about the polyoma virus and how it was beginning to compromise the kidney transplants of "certain patients." It turned out that most of those "certain patients" were black people in places such as Baltimore who were taking Cell-Cept as an immunosuppressant drug. My Georgetown doctors initially prescribed CellCept for me because, they said, it did a better job of preventing organ rejection in blacks, especially when taken in tandem with certain other immunosuppressant drugs.

Blacks routinely have been given stronger immunosuppressant drugs than whites because they often are more hyperimmune. That means, according to clinical experience in the United States and abroad, that blacks tend to reject transplanted organs more quickly than whites.

"The problem is that we tend to rely on ethnic self-identification," Dr. Kopp said. "If a patient identifies himself as black, we don't ask him to tell us what that means." That means ethnic self-identification, in many ways, is a matter of choosing labels. But relying on labels instead of something more substantial, such as genetic testing, to determine the appropriate drug therapies, could lead to bad medicine, especially in the treatment of kidney disease, where race is an important factor.

The nation's kidney dialysis centers are full of black people. I noticed that much in renal clinics in the District of Columbia, Detroit, and New York City. I once asked a technician at Detroit's New Center Dialysis Clinic if only blacks had kidney failure. "No," he said. "It just looks that way."

Blacks account for only 12 percent of the U.S. population, but they constitute 32.4 percent of all patients being treated for kidney disease in the United States.

Black Americans also develop kidney failure at an earlier age than white Americans—at an average age of fifty-seven years old for blacks, compared with sixty-three years old for whites. I was an early starter. I was diagnosed with end-stage renal disease at forty-eight.

Kidney failure doesn't just happen. It often results from other problems, such as high blood pressure and diabetes, the two leading causes of kidney disease among black Americans. There are ten black diabetics for every six whites with the condition, according to National Kidney Foundation research.

Contrary to popular opinion, diabetes isn't the "sugar disease." It's a metabolic disorder that leads to excessive urination, washing away many of the body's nutrients and minerals in the outflow. The disorder stems either from an insulin deficiency, or the body's inability to use ample amounts of insulin available. Either situation allows a critical buildup of blood sugar. Untreated, diabetes could lead to loss of limbs and eyesight, or it can cause critical injury to organs such as the heart and kidney. It's a killer.

I seemed to have developed diabetes after my first kidney transplant largely as a result of steroids administered to prevent transplant rejection. The qualifier is needed because I have a genetic predisposition to diabetes. Both of my parents had the disease. My sister Loretta Marie has it. Many of my aunts, uncles, and cousins have diabetes. But most of my doctors attributed my kidney failure to chronic high blood pressure, which annually causes 34 percent of the new renal failure cases among black Americans. Heck, I have a genetic predisposition to that disease, too.

High blood pressure is the overall leading medical killer of blacks in the United States. Chronic hypertension literally destroyed the vascular system in my original equipment kidneys; it could have caused a heart attack, or a stroke, had it gone untreated.

All of that is bad enough. But several studies also show that blacks are less likely than whites to be diagnosed with renal failure at an early stage. One study cited by the National Kidney Foundation found that as many as 43 percent of blacks now on dialysis only discovered that their kidneys were failing a week before they were sent to the blood-cleaning machines.

My empirical observation supports that finding. It was quite common in dialysis clinics with a predominantly black patient population to see people with catheter tubes in their necks or chests. Those catheters are clear indicators that the patients were rushed into hemodialysis. Ideally, in hemodialysis, patients have vascular grafts in their arms or fistulas in which veins are connected to create a high-flow super-vein. Grafts and fistulas allow hemodialysis to be done more efficiently through the insertion of needles into the bloodstream. But grafts and fistulas take time to develop. It took nearly two months in my first go at dialysis.

But emergency renal-failure patients don't have the time to wait that long.

Blacks with kidney failure also receive more limited medical care than their white counterparts. Although some of the disparity may result from a difference in incomes and health-care coverage, not all of it does. A congressionally mandated report by the National Academy of Sciences Institute of Medicine found that racial and ethnic minorities tend to receive lower quality health care than whites do, even when their conditions are comparable and they have similar incomes and health-insurance coverage.

Part of the problem may stem from the physicians' perception of race and patient competence related to race. Before some Georgetown doctors knew who I was, or what I did for a living, I got the distinct impression that they were talking down to me. It was the same feeling I had when I was a kid in New Orleans cleaning white peoples' houses; often, I was the subject of their amusement because, gee whiz, the little Negro can read.

At Georgetown, an intern in the nephrology department, speaking without intending to insult me, put it bluntly during my very first visits to Georgetown in 1999.

"You are unusual," he said. "You are educated and intelligent. You probably will do okay with all of this," he said, referring to all of the information I had been given about dialysis and transplants. "You are intelligent enough to follow instructions."

The intern was an Asian, a foreigner. I thought he also was going to tell me that I was "articulate," which some non-blacks think is a compliment to blacks, but which most blacks regard as a rank insult. He stopped talking when I asked him if most of his patients were stupid and ignorant. I offended him, and felt good about it. Having my intelligence insulted while being told I had a life-threatening disease really pissed me off.

Disparities in treatment may arise from a number of factors, said Brian Smedley, staff director for the Institute of Medicine study. For instance, blacks living in urban areas may find it harder to get to specialists, who often are located in suburban areas. And, as in other areas of medicine, health-care providers may be too pressured to follow up on the patient's need to be seen by a specialist. Or caregivers may make unconscious race-based decisions about whether a patient is likely to comply with the medical regime, as the Georgetown intern apparently had.

The compliance question is important. Failure to follow the strict dietary and fluid intake regimens required of kidney patients can accelerate kidney failure and hasten the need for dialysis or a transplant. Subsequent noncompliance during dialysis or after a transplant could mean a death sentence.

But assumptions that all blacks need stronger doses of immunosuppressant drugs can be just as dangerous. "Nobody knows or understands exactly why African-Americans reject [organs] faster than whites," said Dr. Clive O. Callender, director of the Howard University Transplant Center in Washington, D.C. Using more aggressive immunosuppressant strategies to treat black patients works for 90 percent of the transplant recipients in that group. For a variety of reasons, that treatment may not be appropriate for others, Callender said.

But doctors aren't treating races; they're treating individuals. When it comes to individuals, the question of race isn't always black or white, even when it appears to be so, Dr. Kopp told me and my family.

Perhaps medical research eventually will lead to the treatment of individuals based on their actual genetic profiles rather than on ethnic labels, which can be misleading, Dr. Kopp said. But when that will happen is anybody's guess.

We left NIH feeling that our time was well spent. Dr. Kopp and colleagues, at some point, would follow my case after the second transplant surgery. We knew that we would have a close follow-up at Georgetown with Dr. Gonin, who is as persistent as Dr. Marcus in tracking patients. But it was also reassuring to know that someone else would be looking in.

[8]

Slicing and Dicing

The Surgery

The surgery started in Martha's operating room with only a minor hitch—a slight difficulty getting the breathing tube down her windpipe. But before the day was over, as *Washington Post* reporter Susan Okie wrote of the near disaster to come, "everyone will be reminded that no surgery—least of all a kidney transplant—is routine."

Okie, who is also a doctor, was in the operating room along with transplant surgeon Amy Lu, two anesthesiologists, and three nurses and technicians to report on the surgeries for the *Post*. (Much of the account that follows is taken from the superb eyewitness account that Okie wrote, augmented by an interview with her, access to her notes, and interviews with members of the surgical team.)

Dr. Lu is a perfectionist, an attractive Bronx-born Chinese American who studied psychology and fine arts at Amherst College and simultaneously pursued a medical degree and a master's degree in public health before she opted to become a transplant surgeon. She did her training for transplant surgery at Stanford. Transplant medicine appealed to her "because I thought it was the most challenging field. It was ever-changing and dynamic because it was new," she said.

Fashionable within the limits of a hospital, she wore a surgical cap decorated with flowers and pandas—but no eye makeup. Martha had complained on the Friday before surgery about not being allowed to wear eye makeup during surgery, chagrined by the thought of being photographed without cosmetic improvement. Dr. Lu had promised to abstain from eye makeup, too, in solidarity. And, true to her word, she had.

The *Post* photographer stepped out of the room while the surgical team took off Martha's gown and got her in position for the surgery. Seven members of the team helped turn her to the right to expose her left flank and belly for access to her left kidney. She was taped in place on the table, with pillows placed under her head and arm. At her head, separated by a drape from the surgical field, her anesthesia team continued to administer drugs and monitor her pulse and blood pressure.

Martha's abdomen had been scrubbed with Betadine. Dr. Lu grabbed a sterile marker to plot her way into Martha's body, making dots on her abdomen for the three tiny cuts where the camera and instruments would enter and a larger, horizontal line on the lower abdomen marking the site of the incision, about three and a half inches below the navel, through which the kidney would be delivered.

The surgery was laparoscopic. Dr. Lu manipulated her instruments through two of the ports while watching camera images on the screen. The technique is designed to keep cutting and bleeding to a minimum to reduce risk and speed recovery. The laparoscopic technique was invented in the late 1980s. Initially, it was used exclusively for gall bladder surgery, then later for patients with tumors on their kidneys. In the mid–1990s, the technique was adapted for kidney transplant donor surgery as well, with the first laparoscopic procedure performed at Johns Hopkins University Hospital in 1995. Before laparoscopic surgery, kidney donors faced much more invasive surgery that resulted in much longer recovery times. Harvesting the kidney back then required a ten-inch incision at the twelfth rib, and the rib itself was often removed. Complications included hernias and damaged lungs, which could be repaired, and an irreparable, painful, debilitating compression of the nerves near the rib cage.

At 8:25 A.M., with one of Dr. Lu's Annie Lennox CDs playing in the background, the surgeon made three small cuts with a scalpel, through the skin and muscle, in the places she had marked. She inserted six-inch long tubes, called "ports," through the holes to provide passageways for the instruments used in the surgery. Next, Martha's abdomen was inflated with carbon dioxide to create space for the camera to work effectively. If the camera was too close to the procedure, the surgeons wouldn't be able to see. Then she inserted a 13-inch long stainless steel tube, the camera's viewing scope. Okie wrote:

> *Martha's insides immediately appear in vibrant colors on two large TV monitors. The view is gorgeous. The inner surface of the abdominal wall is pink and shiny, covered with a delicate network of blood vessels like a red spider web. There's pink bowel and yellow, spongy-looking fat. The liver appears, rose red and huge. When Lu makes the next opening, the screen shows the abdominal wall from inside being pushed inward, then a pointy instrument poking through the new hole.*
>
> *Now instruments have been inserted through all three*

*ports in Martha's belly. A surgical resident holds the cam-
era in one port, keeping it trained on the area where Lu is
working. Lu manipulates her surgical instruments through
the other two. In her right hand, she holds a remarkable,
recently developed tool called a harmonic scalpel. It looks
like a long metal prod with a short pair of tweezers at the
end. She can grab a small piece of tissue, then cut by using
ultra–high frequency vibration to heat up the tissue in her
grasp until it falls apart. The harmonic scalpel cuts with a
minimum of bleeding or collateral damage.*

*As she works, Lu periodically squirts in saline solution
and suctions it out to clean blood from the area where she is
cutting. Tiny bubbles stream by on-screen as she uses a
retractor to push the large intestine out of the way so she
can see the kidney. Kidneys are vital to life, and the body is
engineered to protect them from harm. The left kidney,
looking bluish-purple on the screen, hugs the upper back
wall of the abdomen, wrapped in fat and tacked firmly in
place with layers of connective tissue. Freeing it will be like
using chopsticks for the next couple of hours to remove multiple layers of tissue paper around a thoroughly wrapped
present.*

In an interview months later, Dr. Lu noted that she is
considered the "most minimally invasive" member of the

surgical team because she has small hands. As a result, she specializes in surgery on donors. The surgery on donors requires working in tight spaces because of its minimally invasive nature, watching the procedure on a television screen as she manipulates the instruments inside the body. The once-removed nature of the operation can be stressful, she said, because "you don't have much control in the sense of having your hands in someone's belly."

The recipient's abdomen is open wide with the skin and the fat peeled back like the pages of a book so that the surgeons can reach in with their hands to move things around and do the plumbing required to connect the new kidney.

Carefully, Lu peels away connective tissue and strips away fat. As more of the kidney comes into view, the screen shows the paired artery and vein that bring blood to the kidney and take it away. They emerge side by side from the kidney's inner curve. The artery is pulsating gently. Lu's skill in freeing and cutting these two blood vessels will be crucial to the transplant's success, because they must be connected to large vessels in Warren's abdomen to keep the transplanted kidney alive and working.

The pale pink spleen keeps edging onto the left side of the screen like an extra looking for a bigger part in the production, and Lu keeps pushing it out of the way. She employs the harmonic scalpel and other instruments to carefully remove connective tissue overlying the kidney and expose the blood vessels. She does most of the work by parting tissues gently, without cutting; whenever the harmonic scalpel beeps into action, the sound is almost a surprise.

Lu uses an instrument a bit like a long, thin staple gun to close off a little vein branching from the main vein draining the kidney. "Tell Dr. Johnson that the vessels are exposed and to bring down the [other] patient," she orders a nurse.

The kidney's vein and artery are now clearly visible. At one side of the operating room, an assistant pounds on congealed ice chips and fills a steel basin with iced saline solution to receive the kidney. Lu cuts some connective tissue off the top of the kidney and asks to have the operating table adjusted so that she can more easily work on the area behind the organ.

Now the kidney is almost completely separated from its attachments to the abdominal wall. On the screen, it looks like a giant red kidney bean.

Next door in Operating Room 8, Warren is being put to sleep. At 10:25, transplant surgeon Scott Batty, a large, cheerful man, pokes his head through the connecting door to announce that they're about to start.

Donald Scott Batty has performed or assisted in hundreds of liver and kidney transplants. Born in Rhode Island and reared mainly in Connecticut, he attended medical school at Tufts University in Boston on an Army scholarship, fulfilling his residency at Walter Reed, where he returned later to head the liver transplant program. All of the doctors in Georgetown's transplant center routinely perform both liver and kidney transplants.

A few minutes later, Lu is ready to make the incision in Martha's belly through which she'll deliver the kidney. "Lights up. Gas off," she says. "Got the ice basin and everything?"

At 10:35, she makes an incision through skin and muscle on the horizontal line she has drawn low on Martha's abdomen and inserts a fourth port through the peritoneum, the delicate inner lining of the abdominal cavity. Next door, Batty is cutting a matching line in the skin of Warren's abdomen. But in his case, the incision is much larger, perhaps eight or nine inches long. It will be spread apart by a large, circular steel retractor to give Warren's surgeons access to a wide area inside his abdominal cavity. There, they will prepare a bed for the new organ.

Now Lu needs to make final preparations for the removal of Martha's kidney. She instructs an assistant to hold tight to one of the ports while she moves the stapling instrument in and out through it. She advances the stapler and staples shut the ureter, the tube that carries urine from the kidney to the bladder. Then she cuts the ureter and pulls up on the kidney.

"Bag, please."

Lu takes a furled plastic bag with a hoop attached to its mouth, rather like a collapsible butterfly net. She passes it through the port in the abdominal incision and works it up and around the kidney until the organ is inside the bag, its two blood vessels sticking out.

Quickly she staples the kidney's artery in two places and cuts it. The vein is next. The stapler misfires. "Dammit, this is not on right. Get me the clip applier quickly." She clips the vein, cuts it and rapidly pulls out the bagged kidney through the abdominal incision. She dumps it out of the bag into the waiting basin and sprinkles a handful of ice over it.

"Sew it up," she orders her surgical resident, referring to the incision in Martha's abdomen. She runs with the basin bearing the kidney into the operating room next door.

Later she would return to Martha's operating room to inject a long-lasting anesthetic into the muscle where the kidney had been attached to minimize Martha's postsurgical pain.

While Okie was reporting from the operating room,

Frank was filing live updates to editor Jill Dutt in the newsroom, who was publishing surgical bulletins for the *Washington Post* staff.

Dutt Dispatch, 12:15 P.M.: "Frank Swoboda just called from Georgetown Hospital to report the first stage of the operation went very well. Martha is now in the recovery room and the surgery to remove her kidney went very well. The second surgical team is now implanting Martha's kidney to Warren. Everything looks great. Warren will be in surgery for the next 90 minutes or so. I'll let you know when I get the next update."

That time estimate turned out to be wildly optimistic. Meanwhile, Martha's kidney was in transit.

Lynt B. Johnson, chief of the transplant division at Georgetown, receives the kidney and lowers it tenderly onto a table covered with sterile drapes. Using a syringe, he injects a clear preservation solution through the artery into the kidney to flush out Martha's blood and to protect the organ.

The kidney turns pearly gray as its small blood vessels fill with the solution. Johnson places it in a fresh bowl of iced saline. He delicately cleans bits of fat from the renal artery and vein, each about the size of a soda straw, to prepare them for the transplant. Meanwhile, Lu has gone back to Operating Room 6 and is finishing up Martha's surgery.

Johnson finishes getting the kidney ready and carries it, wrapped in gauze, to the operating table where Batty lays it into the large opening in Warren's abdominal cavity. Unlike Warren's own kidneys, this one will lie just under the skin in the lower left corner of his belly.

Using very fine thread, Batty begins suturing. The transplanted kidney's artery will be connected to Warren's iliac artery and the new kidney's vein to his iliac vein—large vessels in the lower abdomen that supply circulation to his left leg. The surgeons do not plan to remove the kidney previously donated by Warren's wife, which is no longer functioning but remains in place on the right side of Warren's lower abdomen. In addition, he still has his own kidneys. Surgeons do not remove kidneys that have failed unless there is some reason to do so, such as persistent infection, because taking them out increases the surgical risk for the transplant recipient.

That means the new kidney has to be placed somewhere a kidney doesn't normally go, which is fine as long as it is correctly attached.

Johnson and Batty, assisted by chief resident Chuck Cappadona, first work on connecting the renal vein, and then move on to the artery. The big iliac vessels are clamped to keep them from bleeding while the surgeons cut and sew the connections. Warren's anesthesiologists give him drugs and fluid that will maximize the blood flow through the transplanted kidney.

The surgeons finish sewing the connections. The organ "should start working immediately—three to five minutes" after it is connected to Warren's circulation, Johnson tells medical student Jennifer Green. He leaves Batty and Cappadona to finish the case.

Batty unclamps the iliac vessels and the kidney immediately turns pink, a good sign. He picks up the kidney's ureter and trims the end that he will attach to Warren's bladder. He cuts through the outer muscle layer of the bladder at the spot where the ureter of the new organ will be connected.

But suddenly the kidney has turned pale, with blue spots in areas where small arteries have gone into spasm. Batty worries that the color indicates diminished blood flow. He pours a little warm saline on the organ.

"Hmmm," he says. Maybe the organ is in a bad position, kinking the artery. He asks Lu to scrub in on the case and take a look at the renal artery.

They call for a Doppler, a sort of microphone that magnifies the sound of blood rushing through vessels. Applied to the kidney, the instrument makes rushing and whistling noises but not a clear pulsing beat.

Lu suspects that the sewn connection between the donor's and recipient's arteries should be improved. She calls Johnson back and the three surgeons discuss what to do. Johnson, the most experienced member of the team, believes the renal artery has reacted to being handled and sewn by going into temporary spasm. "I think you've got to wait and see what happens," he says.

The surgeons inject drugs, verapamil and papaverine, to dilate the artery. They listen with the Doppler. Johnson leaves and Batty goes back to connecting the ureter to the bladder. By the time he finishes, the kidney is pink and the pulses sound better. Johnson was right: The problem seems to have corrected itself. At Lu's suggestion, they leave the wound open with the kidney in place for 15 minutes and check with the Doppler once more.

"He's happy," Batty says, satisfied.

By now it's after 2 P.M. Batty begins closing the inner layer of Warren's wound, the muscles of the abdominal wall.

Batty has placed the first few sutures when suddenly, without warning, Warren coughs. The kidney pops out of the wound like a jack-in-the-box, coming to rest on the skin.

"Oh, that was not good," Batty says in alarm. As if in response, blood begins to well up inside Warren's abdomen.

———

The kidney's sudden movement has partially torn the connection where its vein is sewn to Warren's iliac vein. Batty asks a nurse to page Johnson and Lu. Nurses and technicians rush back and forth with instruments and equipment. Batty and Cappadona, the chief resident, suction blood from the abdomen and call for fresh gauze pads. Jeffrey Plotkin, the anesthesiologist, sharply orders the anesthesiology resident who has been assisting him to leave the operating room. Then he calls for a unit of blood and starts transfusing Warren.

It was a bad moment for Dr. Batty. It was his first operation as a full-time surgeon at Georgetown. He "wanted everything to go absolutely perfectly," he said. And now it wasn't. Instead of finishing up the operation, he was calling for another basin with ice and saline "in case I have to take this kidney out."

"I think I'm going down to chapel as soon as we finish," he said, according to Okie's notes.

Okie suddenly feared she might be writing something other than a success story involving two colleagues. "I backed off at that point because Dr. Batty was really concerned and paging people and moving fast," she said. "I thought, 'Oh, God, I wish I had not agreed to do this story. I don't want to be here. I don't want to be seeing this. I don't want to be writing this. I don't want to watch this thing go south.' I was really scared."

"When it was over, I was glad I was there."

For Okie, it underscored the fact that nothing in surgery is routine. "It seems like just putting in a battery. You put it in, and it's going to be fine," she said. "But it's so obvious in watching this that a kidney is a living thing."

The drama also proved that it takes a certain type of personality to keep going when things go wrong in surgery.

No one on the surgical team had ever had to deal with an ejected kidney. But they weren't rattled when it happened. They focused on how to fix it.

Within a few minutes, Batty and Cappadona think they have the bleeding under control and try again to close the wound. But some bleeding persists. Johnson returns, scrubs in and helps to place sutures to stop it, explaining later that the renal vein was still leaking at the connection.

Plotkin said later that the cough occurred because the level of anesthetic drugs used to paralyze Warren's muscles had fallen too low. Assuming that the operation was almost over, the anesthesiologists had tried to avoid giving him additional doses. Although Warren was still unconscious, his gag reflex became activated by the tube in his throat, triggering the cough.

Deciding when to start reducing the level of anesthesia toward the end of an operation "is sort of a judgment thing," Plotkin said. It's "like landing an airplane. You don't just go from 30,000 feet to the ground. . . . Part of the art of medicine is coming in for that nice, smooth landing."

Dr. Plotkin, an athletically built Baylor Medical School graduate, said it was several weeks before he could sit down with the resident who ratcheted down the anesthesia too fast because he was initially too angry. But eventually he did. "Yeah, you need to make it a learning experience," he said, "but at that point in time the best move for me and you was to say, 'Get out of the room.'" He didn't want to deal with the resident's explanations while he was trying to deal with the crisis.

The crisis was over, but the operation wasn't.

Warren has put out a little urine, proof that the transplanted kidney is starting to work.

It's after 3 P.M. The surgeons lay the kidney back in the abdominal cavity, but its color turns pale again. They shift its position more vertically and move it lower into the pelvis. If the blood flow isn't good, it won't work well.

Batty and Cappadona close the inner layer of the wound. Johnson asks a nurse to have an ultrasound machine brought to the operating room to get an image of the kidney's circulation. By now the afternoon shift has come on duty and new nurses and technicians have replaced several of the team's members.

Radiologist Doug Jones arrives with the ultrasound device. Johnson tells him, "We've had some questions about the artery, and in the end we had some questions about the vein."

Jones puts a sterile plastic sleeve over the ultrasound's transducer and applies it to the skin over the kidney. From the images on the screen, he can tell that the renal vein is not properly draining blood from the organ.

Johnson reopens the wound. When the surgeons pull the kidney partway out, the blood flow immediately is restored. The challenge will be finding a position inside the tightly packed abdominal cavity where the vessels can function just as well.

The surgeons decide to cut some of the connective tissue binding Warren's iliac vein in place and to shift it upward into the abdomen as much as they can. With that adjustment, the kidney's circulation improves. The ultrasound image shows good blood flow with the kidney in place.

At last, at 4:36 P.M., they close the wound.

What had looked like 90 minutes in the afternoon had turned into a long day's journey into night. Dutt reported to the *Post*'s staff at 7:35 P.M.: "Warren is fine, but the surgery had some complications so it took longer than expected. The surgeons finished a little before 6 P.M. and declared the operation a success. Warren is now recovering in the intensive care unit."

[9]

Recovery

Martha's Story

The first words I heard after the surgery came from the anesthesiologist: "Martha! Martha! It's over."

It felt like a long time had passed. I thought it was late at night when I finally arrived in my hospital room, but it was only late afternoon. What I thought was the day slipping into blackness was me slipping in and out of consciousness.

JE and Sarah were there, and, by the time I was conscious enough to pay attention, the news was good. The operation had been a success.

My memories of the rest of the evening are like short clips of film occasionally lighting up a black background. I had the impression I was asking the same questions again and again. I remember trying not to slur and saying, "I'm having problems being ar-tic-u-late."

The rawness in my throat from the breathing tube was the worst pain I was feeling immediately, thanks to the anesthesia and the painkillers dulling the pain of the incision. Sarah was hovering, making sure I was as comfortable as I could be. My stepson Mark and daughter-in-law Darla arrived, and Mark broke up chunks of ice into smaller slivers that I could suck on, which made it easier to talk.

There were only a few visitors besides family that night. Mary Anne and Kafi came by. So did Susan Okie, who spoke briefly about the operation, but I didn't follow much of it. Frank came by later and said something about Susan being so upset she wouldn't be able to sleep that night. They may have told me about the mishap during the transplant, but if they did it faded into the painkiller blur. As Frank got ready to leave, I asked him to come around to the side of the bed so I could squeeze his hand in thanks.

Even as I passed in and out of consciousness, I was acutely aware that I had an assignment and a story to write. So I turned to Sarah, who wrote the following account as I drifted in and out of sleep:

My mom tells me to get out a pen & paper to take some dictation. I comply, pulling up a chair to her bed. "Okay, go."
I tell her.

She's asleep.

Five minutes later she wakes up—sort of.

"What made me nervous, finally, was so many people working so fast, tying me to the table, giving me anesthesia." She pauses, & I begin to think she's asleep again. The phen . . . painkiller is making her sleepy, & she slurs.

"But I didn't have time for further reflection. I have faint recollection of coming in the OR. By the way, I walked into the OR before surgery."

I knew my mom would be proud of that. They had asked her in the prep room if she would need a gurney or a wheelchair, or if she could walk. She looked at them, baffled. "I can walk," she answered, "unless you guys know something I don't."

My mom speaks again. Her voice is faint, and she exhibits effort with each word. "Then they wheeled me into the Recovery Room. They didn't allow any, . . . " she drifts off. Two minutes later she wakes and asks me what she was saying. I tell her & she continues: " . . . any . . . family . . . in . . . "

"Why don't you sleep now, Mom?" I suggest.

"I just have two sentences more," she says and is asleep again. What a reporter, I think.

A few more quiet minutes, then she reawakens & has me read her the last sentence. "You've re-read that last sentence to me before," she says, looking grumpy.

———

191

"Yeah," I tell her. "You keep falling asleep. Why don't we just do this later?"

"I'm afraid if I don't get it down now, I'll forget it," she says, & continues. "I remember being wheeled into my room, finally. They said it was about an hour later than anticipated. Sarah was right there—no, Sarah wasn't there—they rolled me onto the bed, which was pretty uncomfortable. Then JE & Sarah were there. And Mark & Darla. Since then I've seen Frank & Mary Anne & Kafi. We've declared ourselves 'kidneys-in-law.' I think Mary Anne is feeling better now. I told her one of the valuable things her kidney donation did was highlight the issue of the virus, which will now allow them to treat Warren more effectively. I didn't swell as much as anticipated. I keep hearing that I have beautiful kidneys."

My mom makes a noise like she's in pain & reaches for the bedpan. She retches & air bursts out of her. Her eyes are squeezed closed & she gasps a little. I stroke her head and neck, but she tells me to keep writing what is happening in my own voice.

This is the second bout of nausea that culminated in belching. Initially we'd heard that she would be pumped full of gas prior to the surgery so there would be more room for the camera & tools, but later someone informed us that it was actually the anesthesia that caused the gas. I had been *told to expect her to be bloated & huge, but she really wasn't.*

My mom stirs. "At least nobody has said, 'She looks so natural.' I'm going to sleep now. Thank goodness Sarah's here. It means all the world."

John, the med student, comes to look at my mom's urine & listen to her heart.

"I thought the heart was on the left," teases my mom.

John is unfazed. He's put up with some teasing from my mom already. Cathy, my mom's nurse tonight, comes in & tells us that my mother is low in calcium & potassium. The calcium she can add to the IV drip, but the potassium, she tells us, will be a big white pill. My mom's throat is already dry & sore from the breathing tube, and swallowing a big pill sounds uncomfortable.

9:30: Cathy comes in with some potassium for my mother. It's an elixir, she says, not a pill. My mom is visibly relieved. Cathy & I use the sheet to scoot her up further on the bed. My mom sips the elixir & makes a face. "It tastes like the saltiest salt with just a hint of orange. Bleahh!" She drinks the rest, looking physically pained. "It burns my throat & stomach," she says, then motions for the bed pan before throwing it all back up. I am concerned my mother's body had no time to absorb the K (the chemical symbol for potassium), but Cathy seems content.

I slept soundly finally, thanks to blessed painkiller. Then around 3 A.M. I woke up, filled with a sense of elation. I sat up and called to Sarah, jabbing my thumbs in the air in a signal of triumph. "Hand me the notebook."

"I did it! I feel great!" I wrote. The handwriting was shaky, but the sense of joy was clear.

I had expected that Sarah would go home or stay with JE the night of the surgery, but Sarah didn't leave my side. Without consulting me, she had a cot set up in the room and watched over me all night.

It had been a long two days for her. Mark had picked her up at the airport at 11 P.M. the night before, and she hadn't slept during the four hours she was home before Frank showed up to give us a ride to the hospital. As the surgery had stretched into extra hours, she slept briefly in the waiting room. But most of the time she was awake and worrying alternately about Mary Anne and me.

When I had parted from her that morning, I had been perfectly healthy. After the surgery, she was shocked by the change. "You were really out of it. You were barely conscious," she said. "It was pretty intense seeing you that laid out and sick. I had seen you when you had the flu and were hospitalized. But I had never seen you that sick." And in the morning I had been perfectly healthy.

She was in my hospital room constantly, watching over

me, helping me to hold my head up to vomit, washing my face, and worrying about the IV lines. When I slept, she sat outside the room in the hallway to read and write in the light outside rather than risk waking me up by turning on a light in the hospital room.

I realized how fortunate I was. My beautiful, passionate child had survived her hard times to grow into a loving, competent, compassionate adult.

By the next morning, I was slightly less out of it. I was off the painkiller hookup and getting drugs by mouth. The painkiller hookup is a lovely contraption that allows you to administer morphine by squeezing a bulb, although it has built-in safeguards to prevent overdosing. I thought I was pretty tough, but Sarah cheerfully dispelled that notion. She had checked the records, noting that I had requested the drugs by squeezing the bulb twice as often as they were allowed to be administered.

Frank and Jill came by with flowers and books and more details on the surgery the day before. It was disconcerting to hear, but less so because the news about Warren continued to be good.

The steady stream of calls and flowers from friends and coworkers began arriving. Sarah finally fell asleep soundly and slept through the constant parade of nurses and technicians who came in and out. And a flock of white-coated student docs and a supervisor came by with the news: Warren was peeing up a storm with the new kidney, they said. It's working.

When I wasn't feeling like someone who had been beat up, run over, and left to die, I was feeling like a champion.

On Thursday, Thanksgiving, I woke up feeling good. I was expecting to go home that day and I walked up and down the hospital corridor by myself before dawn. I was feeling pretty smug.

Then, about 9 A.M., I was wracked with vomiting—or gagging—since I had eaten next to nothing. Michael Williamson, the photographer, had arrived at the hospital to take pictures of my departure. I tried to be polite and collegial, but then a wave of extreme nausea would wash over me, and I wondered why I had agreed to be photographed when I was feeling like a wreck.

But I knew the answer: It was because it was a good story.

JE, God bless her, walked Michael out of the room and went off to have coffee with him, so I didn't have to pretend to be sociable. And we canceled plans to leave that day.

That evening, Binta, Kafi, and Mary Anne came by the room and persuaded Sarah to head over to the critical care unit where they were having Thanksgiving dinner. I was glad when she left with them. She needed a break. And I was delighted to see the friendship that was developing between Sarah and Binta, two differently wonderful people.

Later they came back with a container of really excellent butternut squash, the only decent food I had in two days. Thanks to the anti-nausea drugs I'd been consuming intravenously all day, I kept it down.

A day after I had expected to leave, the Friday after Thanksgiving, I was ready to check out of Georgetown, but it wasn't as easy or as fast as I had expected. Sarah was supposed to drive up to Cumberland that day to see her dad, who had finally returned from New York. We were ready to leave at 9 A.M., and Michael was back with his cameras. But time dragged on as we waited for clearances and wheelchairs.

Before I left, I went finally to visit Warren. We hadn't seen each other since before the surgery. I was taken aback by how sick and fatigued he looked. I knew my kidney was working in his body, but it didn't seem to have exercised any restorative power when it came to his general health. He put on a good front, because he was Warren, but he had so many tubes and wires attached to him he could barely move. Even so, it was wonderful to see him and hug him and to think that soon he would be much, much better.

On the way out, Sarah, Binta, Michael, and I stopped by the hospital's pharmacy to fill the prescriptions I had been given. It was my welcome to the world of postoperative-donor-land. I had to pay. Then, Sarah drove me home and helped me into the house and up the stairs to bed. It was good to be home.

And in the morning, it was even better. I got up and brushed my teeth in my own bathroom. Amazing how cheerful such a small thing can make you when you've spent a few days in the hospital. And I read the paper all the way through for the first time since the surgery. Someone had called around 9 A.M., waking us up. So Sarah had fixed me tea and a scone and breakfast for herself. Then we sat on the bed and read the paper together before she headed back to her own bed to sleep most of the day.

My longtime housekeeper and friend, Benedita dos Santos, was there even though it was her day off, and—like Sarah—she was taking charge. She said that she would be back again on Monday, a day she didn't work for me, to take care of me so that Sarah could go visit her dad.

My friend Carol Stoel came by with food, and another friend, Kathy Seddon, also stopped by. I was happy to see them both, but after they left, I had a serious sinking spell, falling in bed exhausted. The following day I was worried. My right eye was blurry, and I had a headache, but I wasn't sure if I could take aspirin. And I felt cut off from the hospital's care. The discharge papers said to call if I had a fever, foul discharge from wounds, or worsening pain, but I didn't have any of those. And it didn't make sense to call my personal doctor who hadn't been involved in the surgery.

Fortunately I was able to reach the resident listed on the discharge papers, who answered my questions. But I worried about what would happen to patients who hesitated to call. At the time, I assumed that the hospital didn't have a program for staying in touch with donors because most donors were family members, so they could stay in touch through the recipient. But it turned out that hospitals don't do much follow-up with donors because the Medicare funding—which covers the testing and transplant surgery—isn't available for much aftercare.

It was five days after the operation when my abdomen finally stopped feeling like a taut, fragile, gas-filled bubble and I stopped taking pain pills. I also walked around the block that day, leaning on Sarah and taking tiny, shuffling steps.

The next day, Courtland Milloy's column about the surgery appeared in the *Washington Post,* resulting in a growing tide of letters, e-mails, and phone calls from friends and strangers who wished Warren and me well. The response from my newsroom colleagues was the most surprising. Who knew the newsroom was full of such softies? It was like *Invasion of the Body Snatchers,* where people's bodies are taken over by aliens. "Who are these people, and what have they done with my coworkers?" I found myself wondering.

When Courtland had called me at the hospital to make sure it was okay that he was writing about the surgery, he had said: "You've changed the vibe in the newsroom." I found that hard to believe, and, if it were true, I expected it to be temporary.

With the new wave of reaction to the story, I began to think that it might take longer to recover from the notoriety than from the surgery.

A week after the surgery, Sarah had left. I went downstairs and made coffee for myself, and also grabbed the newspaper. Going up and down stairs had turned out to be less difficult than I had anticipated, but I was still grateful that my next-door neighbors, Hannah Lepow and her dad Les, had been bringing the newspaper up the twenty-nine steps in front of my house in Northwest D.C. and leaving it by the front door.

I was feeling stronger and better able to handle visitors, too. My friend Nell Henderson scheduled the visitors from the newsroom for me, usually two or three at a time, which was a tremendous help. Even when I didn't feel like holding up my end of the conversation, when there were two or more visitors they could talk to each other and keep me entertained.

————

Nine days after the surgery I was scheduled for a postoperative checkup at Georgetown. I had thought I could probably drive myself, but just riding in the car I tensed up against anticipated pain from every bump, so it was a good thing JE had insisted on driving. By the time I had made the round trip, three hours had elapsed, and I was exhausted and had to cancel scheduled visitors.

When we arrived in the waiting room, Warren's daughter Binta, the hard-charging corporate lawyer, was there, curled up in a chair and asleep. When she heard our voices, she woke up and uncurled from around the book she had been reading: Harry Potter.

Warren and Mary Anne had an appointment before mine. When Warren walked out into the waiting room I was shocked by how he looked—so swollen with fluids that I felt like calling him Puff Daddy. And he looked very, very tired. I didn't want to say anything about how bad he looked. Instead I sang at him, playground-like, "I'm recovering better than you are."

And I was recovering well. I saw Warren's surgeon, Dr. Lynt Johnson, that day. He said I was recovering faster than normal, and that was supposed to have been the end of my association with Georgetown.

The rest of the recovery was largely uneventful. I walked as often as I could, but it tired me out quickly. I hated to think what I must look like when I walked, with my slow, small steps. I wanted to carry a sign that said "Recovering from major abdominal surgery," so that passers-by wouldn't think I was just weak.

Eleven days after the surgery I spent the morning on the back porch in the 70-degree weather with my daughter-in-law Darla while my grandsons Marshall and Garrett tore around the yard. After they left, I ate lunch and took a nap. But I had work to do. The story about the transplant surgery was scheduled to appear in ten days, and I hadn't done much but take notes since I'd come home. I wrote, sitting up in bed, with my lap-top sitting on my invalid's meal tray.

As usual, Frank was right in the middle of things. I would write and file to him, and he would make suggestions over the phone. Warren was too weak to work on a computer, so he dictated to Frank. Then Frank would pass the copy to Craig Stoltz, the Health section editor.

That night Warren called. It was a Tuesday night, and he had suddenly been flooded by a sense of relief that he didn't have to deal with dialysis anymore. One of his weekly dialysis appointments had been on Wednesdays, and by early Tuesday nights, he said, he used to be withdrawn, filled with dread. This Tuesday night, he was free, and he was calling to say thank you.

I felt that sense of joy again that had turned out to be the major surprise of the operation. I had been prepared for the stress and the pain and the brief disability, but not for the joy and the huge sense of accomplishment.

My first trip back to the *Post* was in just a little over two weeks after the operation. My friend Megan Rosenfeld was having a retirement party at the *Post* in the evening, so I showed up for that, hoping to slip in under the radar. The party was great, but I tired out too quickly to be able to stay to the end. I went downstairs to the newsroom to my desk to check up on a few things and ended up staying longer than I anticipated as colleagues came by to offer hugs and to chat. But just being there wore me out. It made me decide to err on the side of caution about coming back to work. By a month after the operation, though, I was back. Some days, I left early, fatigued. But within a few more weeks, I was back to my normal schedule.

Warren's and my story, and subsequent appearances on the *Today Show* and *Talk of the Nation,* had prompted a huge, cheerful response from readers, viewers, and listeners. It was heartening, but underneath it all, I worried about Warren, who still seemed sick and tired all the time.

We had a big family dinner for my birthday and my grandson Marshall's on December 21. JE and my nephew Russell were clearly excited about the present they had for me. It was huge, and when I unwrapped it—an amazing piece of work. JE, who had sort of grumpily been referring to me as St. Martha since the surgery, had made a shrine. It was a straw nook designed for a nativity scene. Inside, sculpted by JE out of papier-mâché, was a small statue of mini-skirted me with a halo and a beatific look on my face. In one hand I held a newspaper; in the other a kidney.

JE had already defined the three miracles that it takes for canonization. The first miracle was getting hired by the *Post*. The second was saving Warren's life. And the third was the one Courtland had credited us with—changing the vibe in the newsroom.

A few days later, Warren was back in the hospital, where he would spend Christmas. That took some of the joy out of the holiday, filling us all with unspoken fears. They were allayed with a diagnosis of dehydration and a continuing clean bill of health for his kidney. My kidney.

That was the last of the major scares. A month later he would be back to work. A few months after that, he would be looking better than he had in years.

And I was fine, too. In January, I had come down with the flu. I spent a few days in bed sleeping it off, then returned to work and immediately came down with the flu again. I worried that my resistance had been reduced because of the surgery, so I saw my personal physician Dr. Bryan Arling, who checked my blood counts, my kidney function, and electrolytes. Other than being sick, I was in perfect shape.

And continue to be. The surgery seems in the distant past. The pain is forgotten, as it is in childbirth; Warren's health, Mary Anne's relief, our children's happiness, and my own joy outweigh everything else.

Warren's Story

I remembered very little from the day of my second transplant surgery. I knew the date, November 20, but my memory that night, and the day after, was fogged by pain and drugs.

I didn't feel the pain until I awakened near midnight in the intensive care unit. It was a sharp, searing agony emanating from the new transplant site on the lower left side of my abdomen. It hurt with the slightest motion. I tried keeping still. But my body was on automatic twitch—and cough.

The coughs were the worst. They seemed connected to serrated knives. Cough, cough. God! Each cough tore out my insides. I was hurting too much to reach for the nurse call-button about eighteen inches from my right hand.

Help walked in later through my hospital room door. How much later, I don't know. Intense pain feels eternal. The sufferer feels doomed.

Relief came by way of a nurse with a pretty voice. I couldn't see her face clearly. I wasn't wearing my glasses, and I can't see well without my glasses. But I could hear, and the nurse's voice was pretty and seductive. I remembered that much.

She stood on the right side of my bed, fidgeting with a machine that dispensed morphine at the push of a button.

"Honey, you must be miserable," the nurse said. "You haven't used any pain medication. You've got to be hurting. Are you hurting?"

I almost cried. Instead, I nodded my head, and that hurt, too.

"Honey," she said, putting an electronic fob into my right hand. "You've got to push the button. Push the button. The machine dispenses morphine through the IV tube," she explained, referring to the one inserted into my right arm. "Push the button, honey. That will relieve the pain."

I said, "I don't want to become a drug addict." That must have sounded stupid to the nurse. But in that moment of disorientation, when I was slipping in and out of my past and present, it was to me the perfectly sensible thing to say. "I don't want to become a drug addict."

I grew up fearing and hating drug addicts, drug pushers, and anything and anyone who had anything to do with illegal drugs. It was the one bias Mommie and Daddy voiced repeatedly, enthusiastically.

I didn't want to have anything to do with morphine, not even to relieve pain, not even at the urging of the sweet-voiced nurse telling me to "Push the button, honey."

But I was hurting too much, too long. I couldn't stand it any longer. I pushed the button—and kept pushing it throughout the night.

By late afternoon on the day after the surgery, I started feeling guilty about using every bit of the morphine I was allowed to use. It felt really good to be free of that horrendous pain. But was I becoming a drug addict in a Georgetown University Hospital bed, a bed facing a Crucifix on the wall at that? What would Daddy say?

I asked one of the day nurses, who assured me that there was no way I could become addicted to morphine using the limited doses dispensed through the monitor, which automatically cut off allocations of the drug after dispensing a certain amount. The nurse's explanation gave me some peace of mind. But I couldn't help thinking that I was beginning to enslave myself, to sacrifice my will to morphine.

After all, I had gotten through life without using dope. I didn't smoke marijuana in college—not one joint. The only thing I inhaled was other people's smoke. I didn't drink alcohol until my sophomore college year. It was one or two glasses of beer at an Alpha Phi Omega fraternity party, much to the consternation of Mary Anne, whom I was dating at the time. She hated drugs and drinking and thought very little of men who used them.

Tobacco? I'd tried it three times in the 1970s and early 1980s. But Mary Anne wouldn't allow me to smoke at home, where one of our daughters, Binta, had asthma. Mostly, though, my smoking flirtation flamed out because I was too cheap to buy cigarettes, pipes, and pipe tobacco.

So, this was it. I had to come to a hospital intensive care unit to walk on the wild side. "Push the button," another nurse said after I had lapsed into misguided discipline. I resisted. She insisted.

"Pain slows healing," she said. "The longer you're in pain, the longer it's going to take for you to heal. You're not going to turn into an addict. The doses are monitored. Push the button!"

I pushed it. Morphine in. Pain out. A warm and fuzzy, carefree fade to oblivion. It's no wonder Daddy hated dope.

By the end of my second day in the ICU, I was fully alert and peeing red through a catheter into a bag attached to the bottom left of my hospital bed. You tend to pee red when surgeons do a lot of cutting around the urethra, attach a new kidney, and do other things to cause internal bleeding. The blood has to go somewhere. That it went through my penis into the catheter was a very good thing. So, I peed lots and lots of red. Nurses, adult doctors, and a bunch of kids in white coats were coming into my room and smiling at the bags of crimson urine. They were making pronouncements: "Good" and "Great," stuff like that. People applauding piss. Weird. I wanted them all to go away.

But setbacks kept them coming through the night. I developed a breathing problem. My chest felt heavy. Something was in my lungs. There was a shortness of breath, and I was coughing up phlegm. I thought I might never get out of the ICU, never go home.

But my attending doctors didn't seem particularly worried. A respiratory problem? Yes, they said. But it wasn't pneumonia. Most likely, it was another complication related to the anesthesia. The doctors recommended inhalation therapy. That meant taking another drug, albuterol, to dilate my bronchial tubes. It was administered as a vapor. I inhaled it by mouth via a plastic tube.

The albuterol made me giddy. My voice squeaked and cracked. I felt and acted hyper. Binta and Mary Anne were in my room witnessing all of this, laughing their butts off.

"Now you know why I used to act so strange after using my inhaler," Binta said.

I wanted them to stop laughing. I didn't want anyone telling jokes. It hurt too much to laugh. I would laugh and feel a spear of pain in my lower left side, where the surgeons put Martha's kidney.

I still had Mary Anne's kidney in me, too. There was no need to remove it, because it presented no threat to my overall health. I felt good about that. I wanted to keep Mary Anne's kidney in me—dormant and implanted on the lower right side of my abdomen. That put Martha on the left, which somehow seemed appropriate, and Mary Anne on the right.

Talk about balance! Some men never get in touch with one feminine side. I was in touch with both of them. Oh, shit! Why did I think that? I started laughing, and it hurt!

Doing the surgery on November 20 meant that I would be recuperating somewhere on November 22, Thanksgiving Day, 2001. I figured it would be in the hospital. It was. But the holiday meant that Mary Anne and Binta couldn't stay with me all day. There were things to do at home, where Kafi and Tony were working with Binta's beau, Earl, to make things ready.

People were feeling sorry for me because I was in the hospital on the biggest family gathering day of the year. But I wasn't the least bit sorry. Being in the hospital was better than being in a grave or sitting in a dialysis chair.

Besides, though they couldn't stay, Mary Anne and the girls popped in and out of my room. The lovely Sarah, Martha's daughter, stopped by in the evening while Binta was visiting. It pleased me to see Sarah and Binta getting along so well. Sarah is a free spirit on endless adventure. Binta is pinstriped, uptight, the oldest young woman I've ever known. I suppose it's because she had to shoulder the oldest-child responsibilities that normally would have fallen to Tony had he been able to assume them.

Binta has a comedic side, which she usually reveals only in the presence of immediate family. But Sarah was working some kind of magic. She actually got Binta to laugh and tell jokes. I watched this in amazement, until I caught on. Loosening up with Sarah was Binta's way of welcoming Sarah into the family, making her a sister by transplant.

I was thankful for that and other miracles, especially for the presence of so many wonderful women in my life. They include Mary Anne, Martha, Dr. Marcus, Lydia Bendersky, Dr. Lu, Dr. Gonin, and all of the Georgetown nurses, too. There were Binta, Kafi, and Sarah to thank, and Julia, the dialysis technician, and an extremely intense and beautiful intensive-care nurse at Georgetown named Jude.

I thanked men, too. There was Frank, of course, and Drs. Johnson and Batty. I was grateful that Dr. Batty had kept his cool and didn't go batty during the kidney-plop episode, which I first heard about in detail on Thanksgiving Day. That made it an especially good Thanksgiving for me, even with a hospital "meal" of cranberry juice and turkey broth.

Martha, who also spent Thanksgiving in the hospital, must have been thankful, too. She was going home the next day. She stopped by my room before she left. There were hugs of gratitude from me and my family. Martha didn't have to go through any of this, especially knowing that I could lose her kidney in much the same way I lost Mary Anne's.

Kafi showed up after Martha's departure to take me for a walk around the sixth floor. But I wasn't walking. I was shuffling along.

Hallway traffic was light the Friday after Thanksgiving. Many of the rooms on either side of the corridor were empty. Does illness take a holiday, or is it that patients, if at all possible, prefer to celebrate at home? I guessed that it was the latter. I began wishing that I could go home, too.

But homesickness was replaced by another disturbing development. I was swollen, everywhere swollen. I looked like a black version of the Michelin Man. Most disturbing was that my scrotum and penis were swollen, too. That made walking difficult—like trying to walk with two basketballs between your legs. There was a lesson in this: Men should be careful of what they wish for in high school.

Dr. Batty said the swelling came from the huge amounts of fluids pumped into my body during and after surgery. It would go down in time, he said. Mary Anne was happy to hear that, but she wanted to hear more about the scrotum and penis. Dr. Batty tried hard not to laugh. Those will go down, too, he assured her. Mary Anne looked at me and smiled. Embarrassing!

By my fifth day in the hospital, I had moved out of the ICU into a regular room. I'd also run out of patience. Hospitals are odd. They are supposed to be places of rest, but only the dead rest in them. Take Georgetown. I saw nurses working thirteen-hour days and doctors who appeared allergic to sleep. The young interns were so weary, I almost felt like offering them my bed when they came into my room. And they never, ever seemed to stop coming.

Someone always was there poking, probing, touching, feeling, sticking, or interviewing me. Sometimes, they came individually. Other times, they came in teams. The teams usually were composed of students, who asked the same questions everyday. Georgetown is a teaching hospital, and aspiring doctors need hands-on experience. But, after five days, I no longer wanted to be a part of the class. I just wanted to go home. I got my wish November 26.

Mary Anne and Binta arrived with my hospital liberation clothes—an oversized jumpsuit. That was appropriate. I was fatter than Fat Albert on steroids—swollen with excess fluids. Mary Anne had to help me get into my clothes.

Luckily, the test car that week was a 2002 Buick Park

Avenue Ultra. I had written a number of car columns in advance of the surgery to lessen the pressure of having to write during recovery. But I didn't cancel the test cars, because it's easier to keep them coming than it is to interrupt the delivery schedule and start all over again. Besides, I figured that I could review some models as a passenger, which is why I ordered two months' worth of the biggest sedans available.

There is nothing like riding in a big, soft sedan when you're held together with staples. And there is joy in returning to a well-kept home after a hospital stay. Mary Anne, Binta, Kafi, and Tony all took care of that. They really put the place in order. I appreciated that and told them so. But that simple journey home from the hospital exhausted me. I went to sleep moments after shuffling through the door.

There was no rest for the weary the next day, Binta's twenty-eighth birthday. Traditionally, Binta's birthday is a week-long event. She had orchestrated things that way since childhood. Not a day of her birthday week passed without her saying something about, or asking us to do something in connection with, her upcoming nativity feast. At twenty-eight, she's no different—still the reigning BAP, Black American Princess.

I was in the spirit, but my stomach was acting funny. I was doing fast waddles to the toilet every other hour. But I was determined to have a piece of Binta's cake, especially since Mary Anne was feeling a tad permissive on the occasion. She gave me a sliver of birthday cake after feeding me chicken broth and white rice.

The birthday hurrahs eventually yielded to talk about that day's *Washington Post*. The newspaper published columnist Courtland Milloy's "Did You Hear About Warren and Martha?" column. As a result, the phone was ringing all day with calls from well-wishers; but all I cared about was my family's reaction. They liked the column, but Mary Anne was upset by the public mention of her lost kidney. She was happy that Courtland had indicated that the initial anti-rejection therapy failed, instead of the kidney itself. "I gave you a good kidney," she said.

My stomach was still acting up November 29, the day of my first follow-up visit at Georgetown. I felt miserable and didn't feel like moving. But I couldn't give into those feelings. Too many people had moved on my behalf to get me this far. I wasn't going to let them down.

It turned out that the upset stomach and attendant diarrhea were caused by intravenous antibiotics given to me during my hospital stay. I wasn't surprised or angry. Life is a matter of tradeoffs. Medicine is a part of life. One antibody kills another, and sometimes the victim antibody is an ally to your good health. It's the biological equivalent of

---

friendly fire. The consequence is regrettable, but the overall objective is to find a livable peace. My doctors gave me another drug, Flagyl. It seemed to work.

I thanked God for that. Living with diarrhea was horrendous. Each visit to the toilet was an attack on my dignity as well as my body. People say death is the great equalizer. But the "runs" ruin equally too. Diarrhea entraps, and whether you are rich or poor, you know that you're a prisoner. If you're in a public place when your belly rumbles, you head toward the nearest toilet, regardless of its location. The runs run you, and that's all there is to it. Doesn't matter if you're wearing silk pants or denim, you've got to pull them down and find a space to squat. You can go back to pretending that you're superior, if that is your thing, after the deed is done.

You've got to be philosophical when you're dealing with a major illness, trying to recover from a major surgery, or dealing with both. Otherwise, it's easy to fall victim to despair. The ups never stay up, and the downs seem to last forever.

Thus went my recovery from antibiotic-induced diarrhea. I started feeling lousy again. The diarrhea returned with a vengeance two weeks after it disappeared, and Mary Anne and everyone else in the family was getting worried. My water bloat was disappearing rapidly, but so was any semblance of physical strength.

Mary Anne started pushing me to check back into the

hospital. But I resisted. The thought of going back to the hospital after spending so much time there over the last two and a half years was repulsive. I developed an acute fear of the place. I became keenly aware that checking in is accompanied by the very real possibility of checking out by way of the morgue. I didn't want to go back as an inpatient.

But I didn't speak those darker thoughts to Mary Anne. She's funny. She can do enormously brave and difficult things as long as she thinks I'm okay, standing there with her. But when I weaken, she gets very nervous.

I remember crossing a bridge once on a recreational-vehicle trip through coastal North Carolina. It was an unwise crossing, especially in a vehicle nearly 40 feet long and 12 feet high. The wind and rain were kicking up, and the motor home was like a kite in the wind. It shook and wavered over the bridge. Mary Anne said that she was scared, and I replied that I was scared, too. That was a mistake. Her fear rose in direct proportion to my anxiety. We finally crossed the bridge. After getting to the other side, Mary Anne made me promise never again to tell her that I'm scared. "I depend on you not to be scared," she said then.

I had kept that promise, and I vowed to keep it during the second bout of postsurgical diarrhea, although I was scared as hell. I received little comfort from Natalie, a nurse practitioner who phoned me to report my latest blood-test results.

My blood creatinine level, which indicates the kidney's ability to remove toxins from the bloodstream, had risen to 1.9 milligrams per deciliter of blood from 1.6 mg/dl a week earlier. Creatinine is a waste product generated by the normal breakdown of muscle tissue during running, dancing, or other physical activity. Not that I was running or dancing, mind you!

Healthy kidneys remove creatinine from the bloodstream and excrete it through urination. Faulty kidneys allow creatinine to build up in the blood. At Georgetown and other hospital labs, a normal creatinine range is 0.6 to 1.2 mg/dl for two kidneys.

I had four kidneys, thanks to my two transplants. But only one of those kidneys worked. Georgetown's doctors speculated that my creatinine level was rising because of dehydration, possibly caused by the second bout of diarrhea.

Early organ rejection was another possibility. The doctors wanted me to come in for more blood work and a possible kidney biopsy and ultrasound check.

I didn't like the idea of doing another biopsy. The doctors said it was a reasonably safe procedure. But it was still a risky, invasive procedure to me. I thought it would be easier to drink more water to replenish fluids lost through diarrhea.

But it's impossible to drink that much water. I had the

biopsy and ultrasound on December 21; the results showed no signs of transplant rejection or a recurrence of the polyoma virus that had killed the kidney Mary Anne gave me. But the gut infection that had laid me low in November was back again. I was becoming dangerously dehydrated. Two days later, I was admitted to Georgetown for treatment. Merry Christmas!

I returned home December 26 looking forward to the New Year. When you have reason to believe that you might not be around for another year, you're especially happy to see a new one. We didn't have to throw a party at our house. We celebrated simply by being there—together.

By the end of the month, I was on a jet plane going to cover a meeting of the National Automobile Dealers Association. It was my first business trip since the Martha transplant.

Mary Anne, Martha, and Frank all gave me the usual warnings. I listened. I appreciated their concern. I promised to obey, and I meant it. But I was hitting the road, baby! There was overwhelming joy in that. I mean, yeah, it was great to be healthy again. But being healthy just for the sake of being healthy never did it for me. I've always needed something to do, always needed a reason to roll. It was good to be back in business.

[10]

The Parts Department

Less than six months after the surgery, we were busy researching kidney disease for our book. Falling back into our habits as reporters, we were interviewing specialists, reading medical histories, and researching Web sites. But it wasn't just a clinical exercise. In the midst of our research, Warren's nephrologist expressed concern about repeated fluctuations in his creatinine levels and ordered yet another biopsy to make sure that there was no virus or any other condition threatening his new kidney.

On May 28, Warren reported for the biopsy. His anxiety turned to anger when he was forced to wait through two hours of bureaucratic delays for the procedure to begin. He was given a sedative a few minutes before the biopsy began.

In a surgical cubicle, a nurse inserted an IV into Warren's left arm and started a saline drip. Then she wheeled him into a different cubicle for an ultrasound to locate the kidney. "Is the new one on the left side or right side?" the radiologist asked. Warren used exaggerated gestures to emphatically indicate "the left side."

That done, Dr. Gonin and an attending physician got down to work, first apologizing for the difficulties Warren had gone through in being admitted for the biopsy. They inserted a long probe through Warren's abdomen, through layers of flesh, using ultrasound to guide it to the kidney. Then, ordering Warren not to breathe, they snipped tissue samples. The procedure was over in twenty minutes, but Warren was kept overnight.

Normal routine is to keep a biopsy patient for six to eight hours to make sure there is no internal bleeding. But even after Warren's urine tested clear, he was held overnight as a precaution.

Warren went home the next morning and spent much of the day in bed, recovering from the biopsy. He also was depressed about having to stay in the hospital again, which had rekindled his fears.

The next day we were back to reporting, combing

through medical reports at Georgetown and trying to get a better picture of how we were cross-matched. After seven folders full of medical records failed to produce an answer, we drove back to Warren's house to pursue more reporting and writing.

Warren's son Tony was in the driveway when we arrived. "Dr. Gonin called, Dad, and she said it was important."

Seconds later, we were in the house and Warren was on the phone, asking for Dr. Gonin. "She said it was important," he said to a secretary, his voice reflecting the stress we both were feeling.

Dr. Gonin's first words were, "Hi, I've been trying to reach you all afternoon," raising Warren's anxiety level. But the news was good. The biopsy was clean. There was no virus. There was no sign of rejection. And Warren's creatinine level had fallen from 1.6 to 1.4. Warren's voice on the phone underwent a dramatic change with the news. You could hear the stress fall away. We went back to writing.

Warren was unusually lucky. In the space of two years, he had received two kidneys from living donors. Many patients with end-stage renal disease aren't that fortunate. There are approximately 52,640 Americans waiting for kidney transplants, and in 2001, 2,025 kidney patients died waiting.

Warren was the beneficiary of a trend in organ transplants, the growing number of organs donated by living donors—usually family or friends. In the same year our surgery occurred, the number of living donors surpassed the number of cadavers used for transplants for the first time in history. Donations from living donors increased by 14 percent that year, compared with a slight rise of 1.5 percent in donations of kidneys from the deceased. But the demand for kidneys has grown far faster than the supply, both because of an upsurge in the disease and the aging of the baby boomers, who are entering the years when kidney disease becomes more common.

Warren was also the beneficiary of decades of medical progress in the field of organ transplants—all of which happened in our lifetimes. If Warren had developed the same disease in his twenties, he would have died.

The first human kidney transplant was performed by Dr. Joseph P. Murray, who transplanted a kidney from one identical twin to another in 1954. Dr. Murray was awarded the Nobel Prize for his pioneering work more than three decades later in 1999. But at the time of the revolutionary operation, transplanting organs seemed like science fiction to many and morally suspect to others.

At the time the historic transplant occurred, Dr. Murray and others at Peter Bent Brigham Hospital in Boston had perfected surgical techniques for transplanting kidneys in dogs and believed the technique would work in humans.

But a huge hurdle remained. Immunosuppressant drugs had not yet been developed to prevent or forestall the rejection of transplanted organs. As a result, it made little sense to subject either would-be donors or recipients to the inherent risks of surgery.

Then fate intervened in the form of identical twins, Richard and Ronald Herrick. Richard was suffering from chronic nephritis, a potentially fatal inflammation of the kidneys. Ronald wanted to donate a kidney, and since he was genetically identical to his brother, it presented an opportunity to try the surgical technique on humans with a greatly reduced risk of transplant rejection.

The case raised questions that remain at the center of concerns today about the ethics of using organs from living donors—how to help the transplant recipient without needlessly harming the donor.

The operation was historic, but something of an anomaly. There followed subsequent operations on other sets of identical twins, but the utility of the surgery continued to be limited because of the problem of immune-system rejection of transplanted organs.

From 1954 through 1963, there were "only isolated attempts at transplantation," according to Francis L Delmonico, professor of surgery at Harvard Medical School and director of Renal Transplantation at Massachusetts

General Hospital. Later in the 1960s, there was some progress in suppressing the immune system to prevent rejection, and also the discovery that rejection could be reversed.

In the 1970s, kidney transplants were being done more often. But transplant rejection rates were high. Only 30 to 40 percent of the transplanted kidneys lasted as long as a year, Delmonico said. Transplant retention rates increased in the 1980s, largely because of the introduction of cyclosporine, a new anti-rejection drug. In that decade, there were 81,283 kidney transplants, according to the United Network for Organ Sharing.

But it was not until the 1990s, with the development of even more effective immunosuppressant drugs, that kidney transplants became a standard procedure for treating end-stage renal disease. The number of transplants doubled in the 1990s, and it is expected to double again in the first decade of the twenty-first century.

Four factors have contributed to the rapid rise in the number of transplants—improvements in immunosuppressant drugs, an expanding pool of donors, the recognition that transplants are superior to dialysis in saving lives, and improved surgical techniques that pose fewer risks to the donor.

They all work together. The rapid improvement in the

ability of drugs to control rejection helped increase the pool of potential kidney donors. No longer do you need to be identical twins—or even kin. We were not an ideal match, but we were close enough. None of the six cell-surface proteins tested for tissue typing was a match, but our blood types were compatible. Warren's blood type is B; Martha's is O negative, the universal donor type, compatible with any other.

"Over the last eight or ten years, the concept of non-related donors has really opened up the ability to get more transplants done," said Dr. John P. Roberts, professor of surgery and chief of the Transplant Service Liver and Kidney Transplant Programs at the University of California, San Francisco.

"The results are better with living donors than with cadaver donors, even among non-related donors, because the kidney is used when it's fresh," Dr. Roberts said. "Cadaver kidneys typically are stored 16 to 24 hours, and that's enough time to lead to some injury," which could trigger an immune reaction and lead to an earlier transplant failure.

Dr. Roberts said that there has also been an expansion of the philosophy about who stands to benefit by donating a kidney. The medical community has realized that, next to the patient, the person often most negatively affected by end-stage renal disease is the spouse. "That's why spousal donation was rapidly accepted. There was a lot of upside," he said. "When people got comfortable with that, then— why not a friend?"

In recent years, the development of laparoscopic surgery has made donors more comfortable with the surgery. Instead of a major incision, the surgery now requires only three tiny incisions for the tools and a slightly larger one through which the kidney is removed.

There's no question that laparoscopic surgery and other techniques have made it easier for the donor to recover after surgery. But some of the statistics and pronouncements by medical providers may overstate how much easier. For instance, both Mary Anne and Martha were told prior to the surgery that some donors recover within a week or two. And Dr. Lynt Johnson, the supervising surgeon for our transplant operation, was quoted in the *Washington Post* saying that, with laparoscopic surgery, "I've had some people who were done on Friday and went back to work on Monday."

There is an understandable tendency on the part of the transplant centers to minimize the downside of the surgery. For them, the surgery and its aftermath have become routine. There's an equal tendency on the part of those of us facing the surgery to want to believe that it will be trouble-free. The two may combine to lead to surprises in the aftermath.

With some donors, particularly if they are competitive, the suggestion that other donors can return to work in a day or two can create subtle pressure to return to work too soon. Mary Anne, an elementary-school teacher, donated her kidney during the summer vacation, but during the first several months of the school year, she was exhausted every day. Martha initially expected to return to work in two weeks after the surgery, but it took nearly a month before she could return to work and nearly five months to return to her presurgical level of fitness.

There are donors who return to work faster, but it may be because of economic necessity. A study by the Living Organ Donor Network based in Richmond, Virginia, found that 42 percent of donors anticipated returning to work within twenty-one days, but only 16 percent actually did. Sixty percent of the donors returned to work after thirty-one days. The study noted that there "appears (via observation) to be a correlation between employment versus self-employed with self-employed returning to work much sooner."

Our surgery was performed at Georgetown University Hospital, one in a growing number of transplant centers in the United States. Georgetown began performing kidney transplants in 1976. Since then it has completed 300 transplants, ours among them.

Like other major transplant centers, Georgetown performs liver and pancreas transplants in addition to kidney transplants. Other types of transplants also are occurring more frequently, including heart, lung, and bone marrow transplants.

Less than two months after our transplant surgery, Martha walked into the newsroom where colleagues were quick to call her attention to a story in the *New York Times* about another reporter, Mike Hurewitz, who had died at Mount Sinai Hospital just three days after donating a portion of his liver to his brother. A subsequent study by the New York state health commissioner attributed his death to deficiencies in postsurgical care. Hurewitz had choked to death on vomited blood in a transplant unit where one overworked resident was in charge of thirty-four patients, according to the report.

Hurewitz's death underscored that while the practice of transplant medicine is becoming safer and more routine, anytime a healthy donor submits to surgery, the outcome could be fatal.

[11]

The Better Angels of Our Nature

News of our operation had become widespread in the weeks before the surgery, despite our attempts to keep it quiet. Word of the kidney donation initially had traveled through the office grapevine via anecdotal reports from colleagues who had spoken to us. One by one, our coworkers would pull us aside in office corridors or come quietly up to our desks and pump us for information. We were reporters who had become a hot news item, if only in the newsroom. It was a role reversal that made both of us uncomfortable.

Although it may seem strange in retrospect, we believed at the time that it was prudent to be discreet. There were good reasons for caution. Warren didn't want to make Martha feel cornered in case she changed her mind. Both of us were concerned with the small but real possibility that the operation might not succeed. We also wanted to keep it quiet because the newsroom culture can sometimes be brutal. It is a skeptical environment in which it is standard operating procedure to look for ulterior motives in good deeds.

"In most newsrooms it is safe to assume that you are more likely to get an elbow from a colleague than a kidney," *Washington Post* ombudsman Michael Getler wrote after the surgery.

And there were deeper, more personal reasons. We were both focused on what we would be going through, especially Warren, who bore the burden of having lost his wife's kidney and now was asking another person he cared about to take a risk to save his life. We only had so much emotional energy, and we wanted to spend it on our families, ourselves, and each other. When you're rewriting a will and making sure bank accounts are accessible in case you die, as Warren was, needless to say, you're preoccupied.

But keeping secrets in a newsroom is impossible, and that turned out to be a good thing. A week before the surgery, our colleague syndicated columnist Mary McGrory made it public. In a speech at a *Washington Post* ceremony, where she received the Eugene Meyer Award for outstanding service, McGrory said: "I am proud to work for a newspaper where friendship is practiced at the highest level. Martha Hamilton and Warren Brown are co-workers in the Financial section. Warren needs a kidney, and Martha is giving him one. I think she is noble. And he is deserving. I want to salute them."

The supportive whispers turned into open cheerleading, which we found more helpful than we could have imagined. By the day of the surgery, we felt as if we were being carried into the operating room on a tide of good wishes from our colleagues at the *Post*. But that was nothing compared with what we experienced after the surgery, both from our colleagues and from people outside the *Post*.

We heard from kidney donors and recipients, from friends old and new, and from strangers. One apparent reason for the huge response appeared to be a hunger for good news and for more evidence of caring in the wake of the September 11 tragedy.

The months preceding the surgery had been a horrifying time. We all needed reassurance that the world wasn't as awful as it seemed.

What deeply affected us was how our story touched people who said that our experience made them want to do something for others. The possibility that what we had done might prompt other acts of caring was an extraordinary, unanticipated benefit.

These were some of the responses we received:

"You turn on a light in a lot of heads and hearts. I know I will try to be a better person because of you."

"Just when you want to despair of humanity, one lovely human spirit restores your faith."

"I've always felt that friendship is a gift that is given to us to be cherished. What you've done has renewed my desire to be the best friend I can be to those I call friend and who call me friend."

"Both your courage and your colleague's are cause for great admiration. I figure we're the last generation to assume we might end our days with only the organs we were born with. Replacing with spares is getting to be routine. But it still must be a huge challenge to body and soul."

"What an inspiring model for human friendship you have given the world."

"What a wonderful gift you've given us all. You've opened a lot of hearts by being so generous."

We received no negative reaction to our story. But there was an element in some of the responses that revealed lingering concerns about race in America. Some readers and colleagues expressed surprise over the donation of a kidney by a white woman to a black man. Some people believed, mistakenly, that racial differences were a barrier to organ donation. Others were simply glad that our racial baggage didn't get in the way.

———

For us, it just seemed natural. Our differences long ago had taken a back seat to what we had in common. The two of us and our friend Frank were bound together by friendship and similar interests and values. What difference did race make?

"Ms. Hamilton noted in her story that she and Warren were of a different race," wrote Ronald Kisner, a former coworker of Warren's from *Jet* magazine in Chicago. "I must respectfully and prayerfully disagree. They are both of one race: human. With all its frailties. With all its shortcomings. But most surely with all its potential."

We like to think so. But Americans are so accustomed to seeing things in black and white that we are still surprised by people who cross those color lines. Sometimes it seems we remain hopelessly separated by the racial divide. Especially in poor neighborhoods, black and brown children may grow up without ever getting to know a white person. And white commuters will often drive through those neighborhoods and look in those faces and not see the same bright sense of promise they believe they see in their own children's faces.

Our neighborhoods are still largely segregated, many of our schools are either predominately black or white, our churches are segregated, and we socialize separately. Probably the most integrated place in the United States is the workplace. For many of us, the workplace is as important as home. It is the place from which we draw much of our sense of community and personal identity. We often spend more time with coworkers than we do with spouses or other family members. We spend far less time in our places of worship and our neighborhoods than we do in the workplace. And, if we're lucky, we make lifelong friendships there, which is why integration in the workforce is so critical.

If we hadn't met at work, we might never have become friends.

In retrospect, we shouldn't have been surprised that many readers reacted to the racial element of our story. Despite the positive changes that have occurred in our lifetimes, racial divisions still run deep, exacerbated by economic inequality. Blacks who grow up in middle-income, middle-class settings often have the same opportunities as their white counterparts, though racial worries continue to shadow their dreams and accomplishments. Middle- and upper-middle-income blacks often labor under the fear that their gains could be canceled, or might be limited, because of racial bias. They also worry that they might be perceived as tokens, the incompetent beneficiaries of affirmative action gone wrong.

But affluent, successful blacks are the lucky ones. Warren's parents and relatives often said: "You already have one strike against you by being black. Don't make it worse by being ignorant." Too many blacks and other minorities grow up poor in miserable neighborhoods, left behind by the school systems and by other services. They are black and brown, poor, and undereducated—out of the game before it even begins.

Even so, there has been undeniable progress.

Some people may still be racist in their hearts but not in their mouths and manners. Racism is no longer socially acceptable as it was when we were growing up. We've come so far from when it was acceptable to say "nigger" that there is now debate over whether it can even be used artistically in literature, art, and history books. People who once unabashedly flew Confederate flags now fly them with a defensive sign: "Heritage, not hatred." (Others still fly them in the usual way with the conventional subtext: "The South will rise again.")

But the South and our home towns have changed along with the rest of the nation. Houston now has a black mayor, and New Orleans has had three—one of whom actually looks black. And both towns are more ethnically mixed now. In addition to blacks and whites in New Orleans and blacks, whites, and Mexican Americans in Houston, there are Vietnamese, Central Americans, and Yankees.

The *Washington Post* has changed, too. Long after blacks and women and other minorities began squeezing through the barely opened doors of the workplace, barriers remained to our full acceptance. We were paid less, heeded less, and often pigeonholed into beats or jobs that wouldn't have been our first choices. But now even that has changed. It's hardly a cause to look up now when a new black reporter or editor walks into the newsroom. Blacks are an everyday occurrence, just like they are in the real world. Although white males still have an advantage, the newsroom has become discernibly more diverse, along with the rest of American society, and many more opportunities are available for minorities and women.

And the lives of our children have been very different from the experiences of our segregated past. They grew up accepting diversity as a fact of life, expecting to be treated fairly and to treat others fairly regardless of race or ethnic background. They always have had friends of other races. They have experienced racism as the exception to the rule, not as the casual, pervasive norm that we encountered as children and young adults. Warren's children move easily in and around what he often called "the white world." They don't see that world as being separate from their own. Sarah is an equal-opportunity friend and lover who rejoices in what is different.

The power of our story is embedded in the reality that love and friendship proved more important than our differences. It's not that those differences don't exist. They do, and among the many things we have in common is our distaste for the current fashion of espousing "color-blindness." In the current usage, too often it seems to be a way of denying that anyone is unfairly disadvantaged, though many are. Our friendship is based on an acceptance of our differences, not on pretending they don't exist. We celebrate our differences. They aren't a barrier to friendship when you get to know each other as we have.

And for that, we say: Thank you, affirmative action.

Affirmative action has been criticized as a tool of social engineering designed to admit the unqualified. Our experience is that affirmative action works. It opens the door to people with different talents and strengths and fresh viewpoints. The end result is a better workplace and a better product. On a personal level, it creates a wider world in which friendship and good will can thrive.

Artificial? Maybe affirmative action was. But it couldn't hold a candle to the tortured devices that kept us apart during segregation. In the medical area, the absurdities included bans on interracial blood transfusions, separate hospitals where we went to die from the same diseases, and segregated graveyards where we rested separate but equally dead.

Given the times in which we grew up, none of what transpired between us could have been predictable. But times have changed, thank God.

Acts that once would have been impossibilities became facts of life—and in Warren's case, a matter of life or death—as a result of our being thrown together in the workplace.

By the time we were moving toward the operating room, our friendship was as natural as any other. Our racial identities didn't matter; our personal identities did.

We were lucky.

Warren's Aunt Helene Gadison Johnson, of New Iberia, Louisiana, was ecstatic when she heard about the successful operation. "Warren," she said in the loveliest of Deep South drawls, "you mean a white woman gave you a kidney? Isn't that something! Mmmm, mmmm. Mmmmmmph."

She went on to talk about the history of blacks and whites in Louisiana, especially about how whites mistreated "black folks" on the New Orleans riverfront in the late nineteenth century.

"You see, honey, you never know," Aunt Helene said. "God works in mysterious ways. A white woman gave you a kidney. You see why it makes no sense to hate? See why we never taught you to hate?"

---

[12]

Last Words

Martha's Story

June 14, 2002: It's been more than six months since the surgery, and everything is going wonderfully well. Two of my four scars are almost invisible, and the other two aren't very noticeable. Other than the faint scars on my abdomen and the scar tissue underneath, I feel the same physically as I did on November 19, 2001, the day before the surgery.

Warren is in the best health he's been in since 1995, in terms of kidney function. He looks great—much healthier than even after the first transplant when the medication he took whacked him almost as hard as the disease had. He takes a pharmacy full of pills every day, but the balance seems better this time, and he's passing checkups with aces. He needs to exercise more, and maybe he will. But I'm not his nanny—no matter what he tells people at work. He'll have to come to terms with that on his own.

Some things have changed profoundly. Warren and I are closer than we ever were before as a result of the transplant. Most of the time, that's a good thing. But sometimes we need to take a time-out from each other.

And the Elder Pod has changed. In February 2002, Frank retired from the *Post,* though he works under contract, editing Warren's car reviews. He's gone off to his dream job as president of the Herb Block Foundation. On the day he left we had a celebration in the Business section, continuing the tradition that Frank had started when he was in charge. Afterward, at the end of the day, Frank left, having cleared out his desk. Before he departed, he stepped back into the three-desk geography that had defined our world for so long—Frank's, Warren's, and mine. He shook hands with Warren, then he shook hands with me, and I burst into tears. Then Frank walked away, and something happened that I had only seen once before in the newsroom, when Ben Bradlee retired as executive editor. As Frank walked out, a spontaneous round of applause followed his progress across the newsroom.

For Warren and me, Frank's retirement brought a profound sense of loss. We had identified a fantastic colleague, Shannon Henry, who would move into Frank's desk, and we knew that we would stay in touch with Frank. But, still, it was the end of something.

Frank said later that, as he walked out, he thought to himself, "I'll never have that again." And it made him sad.

We still have the enduring friendship among the three of us. But we don't have the easy proximity that allowed us to turn to each other for instant feedback on our problems, for reactions to the joys of life, or for the stupid jokes that got us through the day. Warren and I have that, but we don't have Frank, the third leg of the stool.

Funny, sometimes three-way friendships end up in jealousy or competition. Ours never did. We were a unit. As we were writing the book, Warren and I had a hard time describing how the three of us had become so close. So we made Frank come over and sit down with us for a few hours to talk about it.

It was a very difficult couple of hours because, at the end of it, we all realized that what we were talking about was how much we loved one another. Quick! Kill that sentiment!

Back to the transplant: Judging by the questions I get, lots of folks think that donating an organ leaves you somehow diminished. But it doesn't. I didn't have to change my diet or my lifestyle subsequent to the surgery, nor do I have any sense of anything missing.

In fact, it's quite the opposite. I feel better than before, the possessor of a solid sense of joy about what I was able to do.

When I first thought about it, the idea of donating an organ seemed daunting. In fact, it's not much different from giving blood, except it's more invasive, there's more risk of rejection, and the recovery time is longer. I've learned a good deal more about kidney disease and transplants since the surgery than I knew going in, but I haven't learned anything that made me question my decision.

Warren and I were so fortunate. We had good health-care coverage, supportive family and friends, and a caring employer—the best possible package.

For his part, Warren has stopped dancing with denial. He's showing a greater regard for his own mortality now and taking more care. Good work, Warren—and besides, if he screws around, Mary Anne and I will both kill him.

Warren has this theory about receiving a part of a person's soul with the transplant, so I hate to break the news to him that it's just tissue. Nobody gets a piece of my soul, except my daughter, who has had it since she was born.

But I'm awfully glad Warren has my kidney, and I wish them both long life.

———

At the risk of sounding self-serving or sappy, I will say two things:

One, I have done hard things in my life. This wasn't hard.

And, two, that old business about "for it is in giving that we receive"? Who would have guessed?

Warren's Story

June 15, 2002: I have a cold. But there's no fever or anything, so there's no need to call a doctor today. Still, the onset of this late-spring malady means Mary Anne will be on my case about checking body temperature, blood sugar levels, blood pressure, the whole bit. It's impossible not to be aware of your mortality when you're doing stuff like that.

Otherwise, my health is okay. I pee, therefore I'm free. You think that's funny? One of the first things you learn as a patient with end-stage renal disease is that you don't pee anymore. You don't pee much, anyway. For men, that's psychologically diminishing.

You go into a public toilet at a theater or stadium, and all of the dudes are lined up at a row of urinals whizzing away. It sounds like a bunch of little motorcycles. But you stand there trying to coax a trickle, looking at the wall, looking at the ceiling, hoping no one will notice that your whiz is not even a whisper. You feel inadequate—also bloated. The water is there, but it can't find the light at the end of your tunnel. That's one of the reasons you go to dialysis, to get rid of the "fluid."

When I was on hemodialysis before receiving kidneys from Mary Anne and Martha, all of my body's blood was pumped through an artificial kidney (looks like an oil filter) and plastic tubing to get rid of toxins, extra salts, and fluids. The aim was to maintain a proper chemical balance in my system and to keep my blood pressure under control.

The bottom line is that I had to pee through a machine four hours a day, three days a week. I don't care what kind of pretty face kidney specialists and fund-raisers try to put on it, that ain't freedom, folks. It's an in-your-face deal. No dialysis, you die. No new kidney, you die. It's really very simple.

All of which means that I'm determined to do the right thing now that, for the second time in my life, I've been blessed with the kidney of someone I know, love, and trust. I've hung out with Death. The dude really isn't all that frightening, but he's boring as hell. I'd rather live until I can be assured of better company on The Other Side.

Besides, I don't believe in wasting or disparaging gifts. I never return anything a friend or loved one gives to me. I never abuse it. If I can't use it, I give it to someone else who can. That means that if Martha's kidney is still kicking when I'm not, it ought to, if possible, go to someone else who can use it. Ditto any other salvageable part. Just leave something for the coffin. All life is theater, and surely a funeral needs its props.

In the interim, I have things to do—more stories to write, more people to love, more things to learn. Physical life is a preparatory class for eternity. I'm a slow learner, but I'm catching on. It's all about the soul, I think, which is why I believe that all transplants involve karma.

Receiving something of a person's soul enlarges the spirit of the giver and the recipient. Martha, for example, shares her soul with a lot of people through the volunteer work she does with the District of Columbia's public schools, and through her penchant for being there when friends and family need her. Her spirit is enlarged by that sharing.

Martha shared her soul through a decades-long friendship with Frank and me and, on November 20, 2001, literally through giving me a part of her body. In my mind, that is and always will be a gift of the soul, as well as the body.

I meant what I said when I told the people at the Davita/ Georgetown on the Potomac Dialysis Center that I would not knowingly accept a kidney from a person who has lived a life of hate, or who has been deliberately and habitually cruel to others. Call it stupid, superstitious. I could care less.

I believe what I believe, and I believe that when you accept something as personal as an organ transplant from someone, you accept something of that person's soul.

What can I say? I grew up in New Orleans. My people are into voodoo the way some Texans are into oil.

There is something else: I was reared in a family that hated the very idea of welfare, that always viewed it as being more debilitating than helpful. That background taught me to be independent. It also put me at a disadvantage in dealing with the financial aspects of end-stage renal disease.

It was suggested early in my treatment that I talk to a social worker. I spurned the idea. Only poor and needy people need social workers, I thought. I only had renal failure. But I was neither poor, nor needy. Besides, I had an expensive, "excellent" commercial health-care plan provided through the *Washington Post* and the Newspaper Guild.

My high-and-mighty attitude came back to kick me where it hurts—in the pocket. It turns out that, under federal law, all end-stage renal disease patients are eligible for Medicare. It doesn't matter if you are employed or unemployed. It doesn't matter how much money you make. You're eligible.

That's the good news. The bad news is that if you fail to apply for Medicare, your private insurer isn't going to pay most of your medical bills, and that means your medical provider is going to come after you. I found this out the hard way when Georgetown University Medical Center billed me for $77,000 in charges that my private insurer, Aetna U.S. Healthcare, refused to pay.

Aetna routinely explained its refusal at the bottom of each rejection notice: "Please send us a copy of the Medicare explanation of benefit statement for this expense. When we receive the Medicare statement, we will reconsider this amount."

Translated, the Aetna statement means this: "We aren't paying a thing until we see how much money you—the patient and the medical provider—can get out of the federal government. When the feds pay as much as possible, we'll consider paying the rest. Otherwise, go away and leave us alone."

So, although I'm fully employed and reasonably well-paid—and although I have an expensive, "excellent" commercial health-care plan—I've become a Medicare recipient at fifty-four years old. I felt badly about that, until a young woman in my local Social Security Administration office explained the deal.

"It's your money, Mr. Brown," she said. "We've looked at your employment records. You've been paying into Social Security for more than forty years. The government isn't giving you anything. You're just getting some of your money back."

Now that financial matter has been settled, and I'm feeling happy, on top of the world. It is not so much a matter of having recovered as it is a rediscovery of life and what it really means to be alive. All physical things have their expiration dates. Love doesn't. Love is life.

Acknowledgments

Thanks to Craig Stolz who suggested the *Washington Post* story that led to this book and to Susan Okie and Michael Williamson for their superb work in writing about and photographing the kidney transplant operation.

Thanks also to Jill Dutt, Leonard Downie Jr., Donald E. Graham and the *Washington Post* for their important support both before, during, and after the transplant surgery and while we were writing the book. And thanks to Peter Osnos and Lisa Kaufman of PublicAffairs for their enthusiasm and suggestions on how to make the book better.

Special thanks to news research and news systems for

always being willing to help us find answers and to Shannon Henry, for helping us to find our excellent agents Jan Miller and Michael Broussard. We are also indebted to our surgical team—Dr. Lynt B. Johnson, Dr. Amy Lu, Dr. Donald Scott Batty, and Dr. Jeffrey Plotkin, and to Dr. Joyce Gonin and Marianne Worley of Georgetown University Hospital. Thanks also to the National Kidney Foundation, the United Network for Organ Sharing, and the Howard University Transplant Center for data on kidney disease and minorities.

Thanks to Frank Swoboda, Sarah Hamilton, JE McNeil, Leigh Glenn and Tom Frail for their suggestions on our proposal and the manuscript and to other family members and friends for their tolerance while we were preoccupied with the book. And thanks to Didier DuPoux for his assistance in getting around New York as we made the rounds with our proposal.

We are also grateful to Alice Bonner, LaBarbara Bowman, Dorothy Gilliam, and Richard Prince for refreshing our memories about the Metro Seven.

Index

INDEX

INDEX

PublicAffairs is a publishing house founded in 1997. It is a tribute to the standards, values, and flair of three persons who have served as mentors to countless reporters, writers, editors, and book people of all kinds, including me.

I.F. STONE, proprietor of *I. F. Stone's Weekly*, combined a commitment to the First Amendment with entrepreneurial zeal and reporting skill and became one of the great independent journalists in American history. At the age of eighty, Izzy published *The Trial of Socrates,* which was a national bestseller. He wrote the book after he taught himself ancient Greek.

BENJAMIN C. BRADLEE was for nearly thirty years the charismatic editorial leader of *The Washington Post.* It was Ben who gave the *Post* the range and courage to pursue such historic issues as Watergate. He supported his reporters with a tenacity that made them fearless and it is no accident that so many became authors of influential, best-selling books.

ROBERT L. BERNSTEIN, the chief executive of Random House for more than a quarter century, guided one of the nation's premier publishing houses. Bob was personally responsible for many books of political dissent and argument that challenged tyranny around the globe. He is also the founder and longtime chair of Human Rights Watch, one of the most respected human rights organizations in the world.

For fifty years, the banner of Public Affairs Press was carried by its owner Morris B. Schnapper, who published Gandhi, Nasser, Toynbee, Truman and about 1,500 other authors. In 1983, Schnapper was described by *The Washington Post* as "a redoubtable gadfly." His legacy will endure in the books to come.

Peter Osnos, *Publisher*